THE COMPLETE IDIOT'S GUIDE® TO

Sausage Making

by Jeff King and Jeanette Hurt

ALPHA

A member of Penguin Group (USA) Inc.

To my family and friends who have supported and encouraged me in all of my culinary endeavors. —Jeff

This book is dedicated to Quinn, the light of my life. —Jeanette

ALPHA BOOKS

Published by the Penguin Group

Penguin Group (USA) Inc., 375 Hudson Street, New York, New York 10014, USA • Penguin Group (Canada), 90 Eglinton Avenue East, Suite 700, Toronto, Ontario M4P 2Y3, Canada (a division of Pearson Penguin Canada Inc.) • Penguin Books Ltd., 80 Strand, London WC2R 0RL, England • Penguin Ireland, 25 St. Stephen's Green, Dublin 2, Ireland (a division of Penguin Books Ltd.) • Penguin Group (Australia), 250 Camberwell Road, Camberwell, Victoria 3124, Australia (a division of Pearson Australia Group Pty. Ltd.) • Penguin Books India Pvt. Ltd., 11 Community Centre, Panchsheel Park, New Delhi—110 017, India • Penguin Group (NZ), 67 Apollo Drive, Rosedale, North Shore, Auckland 1311, New Zealand (a division of Pearson New Zealand Ltd.) • Penguin Books (South Africa) (Pty.) Ltd., 24 Sturdee Avenue, Rosebank, Johannesburg 2196, South Africa • Penguin Books Ltd., Registered Offices: 80 Strand, London WC2R 0RL, England

Copyright © 2012 by Jeff King and Jeanette Hurt

THE COMPLETE IDIOT'S GUIDE TO and Design are registered trademarks of Penguin Group (USA) Inc.

International Standard Book Number: 978-1-61564-145-1
Library of Congress Catalog Card Number: 2011912288

14   13   12   8   7   6   5   4   3   2   1

Interpretation of the printing code: The rightmost number of the first series of numbers is the year of the book's printing; the rightmost number of the second series of numbers is the number of the book's printing. For example, a printing code of 12-1 shows that the first printing occurred in 2012.

Printed in the United States of America

Note: This publication contains the opinions and ideas of its authors. It is intended to provide helpful and informative material on the subject matter covered. It is sold with the understanding that the authors and publisher are not engaged in rendering professional services in the book. If the reader requires personal assistance or advice, a competent professional should be consulted.

The authors and publisher specifically disclaim any responsibility for any liability, loss, or risk, personal or otherwise, which is incurred as a consequence, directly or indirectly, of the use and application of any of the contents of this book.

Most Alpha books are available at special quantity discounts for bulk purchases for sales promotions, premiums, fund-raising, or educational use. Special books, or book excerpts, can also be created to fit specific needs.

For details, write: Special Markets, Alpha Books, 375 Hudson Street, New York, NY 10014.

Publisher: *Marie Butler-Knight*
Associate Publisher: *Mike Sanders*
Executive Managing Editor: *Billy Fields*
Senior Acquisitions Editor: *Tom Stevens*
Development Editor: *Jennifer Moore*
Senior Production Editor: *Kayla Dugger*

Copy Editor: *Louise Lund*
Cover Designer: *Rebecca Batchelor*
Book Designers: *William Thomas, Rebecca Batchelor*
Indexer: *Johnna VanHoose Dinse*
Layout: *Ayanna Lacey*
Proofreader: *John Etchison*

Contents

Appendixes

Introduction

Most sausage connoisseurs remember the first sausage that made them fall in love with sausage.

For Jeff, there were two sausages he made in culinary school. His group was assigned to make a Colombian chorizo. His professor instructed them to only use the spice profiles as guidelines, and his group made the sausage three times to get the flavor exactly right. Then, Jeff and his fellow students got to taste their creations. Sublime. Rich, savory meat, perfectly balanced salt and spice with just the right touch of heat. Jeff had never before tasted sausages so good.

For Jeanette, it was a Spanish chorizo she savored on the main plaza of Toledo, Spain. The sausage was simply amazing.

Those sausages were every bit as complex as an entire dish like an osso buco braised in white wine and served with a rich, creamy risotto. They were so delicious, so good, that we dreamed about them later. Since you're reading this book, we believe you know what we're talking about. You've had at least one sausage that made you swoon, and after you tasted it, you searched high and low to find it again.

But what you may have discovered is that the only way to reach this sausage nirvana is to make it yourself. Artisan sausage making is all about creating the best sausage you can make. When you pursue sausage to the same level of perfection as you do other culinary endeavors, you create art, and art is what artisan sausage making is all about.

In this book, we guide you in your artistic pursuit of sausage. We not only detail the techniques, equipment, and best practices you need to make sausage, but we also encourage you to use your own tastes and flavor preferences to create your own unique sausages.

These days, sausages are booming. They're in fine restaurants, in gastro-pubs and cafés, and they're still standbys at the ballpark. You could say they're part of "the wurst of times." Sausages are also part of the growing interest in organic food and handcrafted artisan products, and people are increasingly interested in making their own links.

But the idea of making your own kielbasa or chorizo might still intimidate you. It's okay to feel a little intimidated or overwhelmed, and you're not an idiot for feeling that way. We both were more than a little overwhelmed and even skittish when we started making our own sausages, and we work with food for a living! That said, after we got over our initial jitters, we discovered two things. First, no commercially produced sausage comes close to the sausage you make yourself. And second, making your own sausage is a lot of fun!

There's nothing more satisfying than using your own tastes to design your own unique sausage. And grilling your own bratwurst or Italian sausage is one of the highlights of any summer day. Each bite tastes more perfect than the last.

We hope you'll discover the same sense of excitement and enjoyment as you learn to make sausages in this book. *The Complete Idiot's Guide to Sausage Making* will have you grinding, linking, and grilling sausages like a pro. Soon you'll be able to make your own sausages for your family and friends to enjoy. Happy cooking!

How to Use This Book

It may be trite, but the best place to start is at the beginning. **Part 1, Getting Started,** covers the basics of artisan sausage making. It not only introduces you to the history of sausage making and the artisan food movement, but it shows you how to equip your kitchen, shop for ingredients, and safely handle your meat. It also fills you in on the proper techniques to make both bulk and linked sausages. After reading this part, you're ready to make all the recipes in this book.

Part 2, Traditional Sausage Recipes, equips you with the basic recipes you need to make bulk sausages and traditional linked sausages. Chapters in this part include recipes for common sausages like Italian, chorizo, bratwurst, and kielbasa. Each chapter also details a bit of the history and lore behind these popular links.

Part 3, Exotic Sausage Recipes, dabbles in the world of alternative sausage making. Instead of traditional pork sausages, here you find out how to make leaner sausages made with poultry, seafood, and nonmeat proteins like soy and beans. Other chapters provide recipes for Asian-themed sausages and sausages made with game meat such as venison, bear, and elk.

Part 4, Cooking with Sausage, steps you through the process of curing and smoking sausages, and offers up many recipes that call for these techniques. It also shows you how to make condiments and accompaniments for your sausages, offers you recipes to use with your homemade sausages, shows you how to pair your sausages with beer and wine, and even reveals to you how to perfectly cook your sausages.

Extras

We have to admit it: we're sausage geeks, and we dearly love to share our knowledge and spread our enthusiasm to anyone who cares to listen. For your special benefit, we've added some interesting tidbits and facts in each chapter, which you'll find in these sidebars:

> **DEFINITION**
>
> Here we define terms that might be unfamiliar to you but are frequently used in sausage and culinary circles.

> **THE GRIND**
>
> Turn to these sidebars for warnings about challenging or confusing details involved in making sausages, with tips on how to identify snafus and avoid them.

> **PRIME CUT**
>
> This is a space for little bits of interesting information. Enjoy the trivia on its own—or impress your friends with these "meaty" details.

> **CHEF'S CHOICE**
>
> Here we recommend substitutions and variations to recipes.

Acknowledgments

This book could not have been written without the loving support of our families and friends. Thanks also go out to Jeanette's husband, Kyle, our photographer; Bec Loss, our web designer and illustrator; Damon Brown, Jeanette's writing buddy; Jeff's sausage making partner, Andrew Waszak; Marilyn Allen, our knowledgeable agent; Chef David Kramer, our technical editor; and our wonderful editing staff: Tom Stevens, acquisitions editor; Jennifer Moore, development editor; Kayla Dugger, production editor; and the other talented people at Alpha Books.

Special Thanks to the Technical Reviewer

The Complete Idiot's Guide to Sausage Making was reviewed by an expert who double-checked the accuracy of what you'll learn here, to help us ensure that this book gives you everything you need to know about sausage making. Special thanks are extended to David Kramer.

Executive Chef David Kramer is a graduate of the Foodservice Administration program at the College of DuPage; the Culinary Institute of America in Hyde Park, New York; and Northwood University.

Trademarks

All terms mentioned in this book that are known to be or are suspected of being trademarks or service marks have been appropriately capitalized. Alpha Books and Penguin Group (USA) Inc. cannot attest to the accuracy of this information. Use of a term in this book should not be regarded as affecting the validity of any trademark or service mark.

Getting Started

This part of the book steps you through the process of making your own artisan sausages. It details all of the techniques, equipment, and safety practices for making delicious links and bulk sausages. Along the way, it explores a bit of the history of sausage making and the artisan food movement in general.

If you've never made sausage before, you should read the chapters in this part before moving on to the recipes themselves. However, if you're a seasoned sausage maker and are already well-acquainted with culinary techniques and food safety, feel free to skip ahead to the recipes in Parts 2, 3, and 4.

Introduction to Artisan Sausage Making

In This Chapter

- A peek at industrial sausage making
- What artisan sausage making is all about
- A brief history of sausage making
- Sausage as a global culinary phenomenon

Nothing says "summer barbecue" quite like a thick, juicy bratwurst boiled in beer and grilled over hot coals. And if that sausage is hand-made in your own kitchen from rich, whole pork rather than produced in a far-away factory from unpronounceable parts and ingredients, you've achieved sausage nirvana. When you make your own sausage, you join the legions of home bread bakers, home cheese makers, and home chefs who are returning to time-honored culinary traditions while taking advantage of today's modern technology and global tastes.

This chapter offers insights into what makes artisan sausages special. We start by explaining the artisan food movement in general. Because the artisan food movement has its roots in traditional food preparation, this chapter covers some interesting points of sausage making history, too.

Why Go Artisan?

If you're like most people, the sausages you've been eating all your life have been made in factories using industrial processes. A commercial sausage company makes sausages that appeal to the largest demographic possible at the lowest possible cost. Each sausage churned out onto the industrial-size conveyor belt also tastes just like every other sausage produced by the factory. So whether you eat a commercially produced brat in September or in May, it's going to taste exactly the same. In order to keep the flavor exactly the same, commercial producers add preservatives to their links, which means that they're never as fresh as homemade sausages. Manufacturers also sometimes add chemicals to their sausages, and there may be some health concerns about the use of these chemicals.

Handcrafted vs. Highly Processed

With *artisan* sausages, the process and the philosophy are different. When an artisan makes a sausage (or any other product, for that matter), he is making a sausage based on his particular tastes. It's as close to perfection as the artisan can get.

DEFINITION

Artisan means hand-crafted in small batches by an artisan or a specialized worker. The term *artisan* also refers to the extra care and attention that is put into the product.

As an artisan sausage maker, you craft sausages in small batches, which means they can have seasonal variations. For example, you'll probably only make some sausage recipes when certain herbs are in season and widely available. In addition, because you aren't using a machine to churn out cookie-cutter identical batches of sausage, each sausage you make will be unique.

Industrial Ingredients

The ingredients used are one of the primary ways of differentiating industrial sausages from artisan sausages. Here's the list of ingredients from a typical commercial bratwurst:

- Pork
- Water
- Corn syrup
- Salt
- Dextrose
- Monosodium glutamate (MSG)

- Flavorings
- BHA
- Propyl gallate
- Citric acid

Let's start with the first ingredient: pork. With artisan sausages, the pork is typically pork shoulder (more on that in Chapter 2) or another specific part of the hog. Industrially made sausages can contain "unmentionable" parts of a hog. It doesn't mean that they're inedible, but it might make you queasy if you knew exactly what you were putting in your mouth.

Not only that, but these pork parts are often removed by heavy pressure and heat. In this process, the meat runs off the hog carcasses in a slurry, or watery mess, and the result is called *mechanically recovered meat* or *mechanically separated meat*. Industrial processors also add ground gristle or cartilage to their products.

The pork comes from hogs that are most likely kept on large factory farms and then sold at the cheapest price that the sausage company can negotiate. An artisan, on the other hand, purchases the best-quality meat he or she can afford. The artisan is also free to choose meat from animals that have been humanely treated.

The second most common ingredient in industrially produced sausage is corn syrup, which is sugar derived from corn. You're not going to find this ingredient listed in any of the recipes in this book. The only reason producers add sugar to savory products like sausage is to improve the taste. But when you make things by hand, using the highest-quality ingredients available, you don't need to make it taste better by adding corn syrup.

As far as the rest of the ingredients, dextrose is another type of sugar, which enhances the ability of mass-produced sausages to brown when fried. Monosodium glutamate is a food additive and flavor enhancer. Again, if you're using high-quality ingredients, you don't need to enhance the flavor. "Flavorings" is a catchall term to describe chemicals that are added to make the food taste better. Even "natural flavorings," while they may derive from real products, aren't the real foods themselves—they're chemicals that taste like certain foods.

BHA, or *butylated hydroxyanisole*, is a preservative that the National Institutes of Health says is "reasonably anticipated to be a human carcinogen, based on sufficient evidence of carcinogency (cancer-causing) in experimental animals."

Propyl gallate is a food additive that keeps foods with a long shelf life from going rancid. Like BHA, it is believed to cause cancer, and has been banned in some countries (though the FDA considers it safe!). Propyl gallate is often used in conjunction with BHA or BHT (another chemical preservative that's suspected to cause cancer) to improve its efficiency at preserving foods.

Citric acid is a natural preservative derived from lemon juice, but you're not going to add it to your homemade sausages.

In short, you practically need a chemistry degree to read the ingredients list of many industrially made sausages. And when you understand what all those strange terms really mean, you might not want to eat the product.

Artisan Ingredients

Now take a look at an ingredients list for a typical artisan brat:

- Pork shoulder
- Kosher salt
- Black pepper
- White pepper
- Rubbed sage
- Celery seed
- Mace

As you can see, artisan sausage contains real foods and ingredients rather than the makings of a chemistry experiment.

Simply put, artisan sausages not only taste better, but they're better for you. When you taste a sausage that's been handcrafted by a butcher, a chef, or even your friend, you taste the care—and the real ingredients—that have been put into that sausage.

The Artisan Food Movement

Over the last decade, Americans have had an increasing appreciation for high-quality products made in small batches. This artisan food movement goes hand-in-hand with the *slow food* movement, the *locavore* movement, and the *organic* food movement.

What all of these food movements have in common is they are a reaction against the unhealthy, fast-food lifestyle.

Artisan food producers and artisan sausage makers fit in with the slow food movement's goal of supporting "food communities who practice small-scale and sustainable production of quality foods." Locavores, people who try to eat mostly locally grown and produced foods, tend to support local artisan manufacturers and producers of foods. And plenty of artisan food producers use organic ingredients.

DEFINITION

The **slow food** movement was started in Italy by Slow Food International, an international nonprofit, to counteract the "fast food, fast life" mentality; it's a big supporter of artisan foods. The **locavore** movement was started in Northern California by two women who wanted to see if they could eat only local products; a locavore is someone who tries to eat foods grown near his or her home. Food that is certified **organic** is guaranteed not to be grown with chemical fertilizers, pesticides, or herbicides and doesn't contain genetically modified organisms.

In a sense, each of these food movements supports the practice of using traditional techniques to make quality foods in small quantities. Each movement also encourages consumers to pause, slow down, and examine the source of their food. Instead of just chowing down on mass-produced, heavily marketed foods, when you focus on artisan foods, you become a bit more thoughtful about your dining choices.

That's one of the main benefits to making your own food, including sausage. Not only can you orchestrate the taste profile of what you eat, but you're in control of exactly where your ingredients come from. You might also be able to have a relationship with your producers, especially if their farms aren't too far away from where you live.

That's the beauty of being an artisan. You can use organic and locally produced spices and produce. You can use naturally raised meat and poultry. In fact, depending on where you live, you can draw on local small farmers and ecologically sound and sustainable practitioners for almost every ingredient you need.

PRIME CUT

One of the best quotes about why to choose artisan sausages over industrial sausages comes from the *Boston Cooking School Cook Book,* which dates back to 1884: "If you like to know what you're eating, have your sausage meat prepared at home or by someone whom you can trust." Amen to that!

A Brief History of Sausage Making

A big part of artisan sausage making involves returning to early sausage making traditions.

Rudimentary sausage making began as early as 9000 B.C.E., when humans started congregating in settlements and domesticating animals. Like many tasty inventions, sausage making was born of necessity. When people butchered an animal, they had all sorts of unused morsels—good to eat, but not big enough to make a whole portion of anything. They were also left with stomachs and intestines from the animal, which they discovered were good "containers" for these unused bits of meat.

Sausage making was also one of the earliest methods of food preservation. The process of stuffing, salting, and smoking meats kept them from going bad. It's interesting to note that dried and cured traditions of sausage making are found in countries with warmer climates—such as Spain and Italy—while countries with cooler climates—like Germany and Great Britain—are known more for their fresh sausages.

The oldest sausages, though, were simple creations. Research says they were just chopped-up odds and ends from the butchered animal, which were then mixed with locally grown herbs, spices, and maybe a pinch of salt, and then thrown into a storage container of some sort. That's the minimum requirement for sausage: chopped meat, salt and spices, and some sort of a container, usually the stomach or intestine of a butchered animal.

The Earliest Records of Sausages

While the earliest sausages were probably consumed by different ancient peoples around the globe, the earliest written reference comes from the ancient Greeks in Homer's *The Odyssey*, which was written in 800 B.C.E. but likely was passed down orally by storytellers for several centuries prior to that. *The Odyssey* describes a type of blood sausage in the following passage:

> There are some goats' paunches down at the fire, which we have filled with blood and fat, and set aside for supper. He who is victorious and proves himself to be the better man shall have his pick of the lot.

The hero gets the pick of the sausages.

A humble sausage seller is also the hero of Aristophanes' play *The Knights*, which dates back to 424 B.C.E. The play describes the seller, Agoracritus, as having the perfect background to become a politician:

> Mix and knead together all the stage business as you do for your sausages. To win the people, always cook them some savory that pleases them. Besides, you possess all the attributes of a demagogue: a screeching, horrible voice, a perverse, cross-grained nature and the language of the marketplace. In you, all is united which is needful for governing.

PRIME CUT

Salami, that delicious, hard cured sausage, is believed to have come from the Greek island of Salamis or from the city of Salamis in Cyprus.

The ancient Greeks didn't have a corner on artistic references to the homely sausage. In China, perhaps the earliest mural of sausage making was painted in the Han dynasty (206 B.C.E.–220 C.E.). These murals depict meats being preserved on a high pole with two rods strung across at the top, from which meat strips, intestines, and stomachs are hung.

Then, of course, there are the Romans. Not to be outdone, the Romans smoked their sausages, sought out new spices and ingredients to add more zip to them, and taught the art of sausage making to the peoples in their conquered territories. In fact, our word *sausage* comes from the Latin word *salsus*, which means "salted."

Ancient Roman gourmands also wrote one of the world's first cookbooks, the *Apicius*. Named for one of two gourmets of the same name in about the fourth or fifth century C.E., it dedicates an entire chapter to the art of *forcemeats*.

DEFINITION

A **forcemeat** is a type of ground meat that is blended with fat. It can refer to a sausage as well as a pâté or terrine.

The recipe book includes a recipe for lucanicae, an ancient Roman sausage believed to have origins in Southern Italy. The lucanicae contained pepper, cumin, savory, rue, parsley, bay berry spice, and an ancient Roman fish sauce called liquamen. The meat, combined with these spices, was then mixed with whole peppercorns, fat, and pine nuts before being stuffed into intestines and smoked.

The *Apicius* also contains a recipe for blood sausage, as well as a sausage that is linked, shaped into a ring, and then smoked.

Further advances in sausage making didn't really take place until the Crusades and their aftermath. The Crusades exposed Europe to the wonderful spices of Asia, and the new spices introduced by the Spice Trade made their way into many traditional sausages. Instead of making do with local herbs, sausage makers could add exotic spices like cinnamon and ginger to their links. In a sense, the Spice Trade was the first form of global fusion cuisine!

The Middle Ages and Renaissance

Sausage making continued to evolve throughout the Middle Ages. A guide for proper medieval women published in the late 1300s, *Le Menagier de Paris*, suggests making blood sausage by mixing leftover blood from a butchered pig with fat, minced onions, salt, ginger, cloves, and pepper. This lovely journal also includes one of the first recipes for andouille sausage. Though andouille now usually refers to a type of Cajun pork sausage, its origins are French.

As the Middle Ages gave birth to the Renaissance period, sausage making became more of an art, with specialized butchers as the practitioners. Sausage making was so prevalent that certain towns—Bologna, Vienna, and Frankfort, among them—had locally made sausages named after them. "Forced meat" or "forc'd meat" sausages were quite popular, and they were highly spiced culinary endeavors. People ate them with wines, ales, and beers, a tradition that continues to this day.

During this period, the system of guilds, or advanced trades, was fully in place, and people who made and sold sausages or prepared meats were restricted by the guilds. In France, for example, sausages were the domain of *charcutiers* or meat preparers, who owned *charcuteries*, or prepared meat shops.

DEFINITION

Charcuterie comes from the term *char cuit*, which means "cooked flesh." A **charcutier** is someone who prepares cooked meats, especially pork; a shop selling these prepared meats is a **charcuterie**. Today, charcuterie includes sausages, pâtés, terrines, and cured meats.

In the 1400s and 1500s, the French government strictly divided the tasks of killing the animals, cutting up the carcasses, and cooking the meat into sausages among fisheries, slaughterhouses, butcher shops, and charcuteries because of illness and diseases.

Charcutiers didn't like not being able to process their own meats, so they rebelled, and eventually, by the 1600s, they were able to process their own meats, and they continued to improve upon the flavors of their products, including sausages.

During this time, linked sausages evolved from a single, cooked coil of sausage from which individual portions were broken off into individual links that were formed and cooked separately.

And sausages also continued to be mentioned in literature, including, of course, by a certain William Shakespeare. In his comedy *Twelfth Night*, Fruella, a rival hotel keeper says to L'Agiato, "I will give you the best of Lombardy; partridges, homemade sausages, pigeons, pullets and whatever else you may desire."

Sausage making, of course, spread to "the New World" with English and Spanish explorers and settlers bringing along their sausage making traditions. The traditional American breakfast sausage came with the early colonists. Made of ground pork, salt, black pepper, and sage, this sausage remains a popular breakfast staple to this day.

French, Dutch, Italian, and Polish immigrants brought their sausage making traditions to the United States. These European sausage traditions were matched by the meat preservation techniques of Native Americans, who made venison and buffalo jerky as well as pemmican, a mixture of venison or buffalo meat, fat, berries, and herbs, which is then packed into animal hide containers.

By the eighteenth and nineteenth centuries, the sausages and the recipes were pretty similar to the sausages and sausage-inspired dishes that we eat today.

PRIME CUT

One of the best quotes about sausage hails from Otto Von Bismarck, the German Prussian statesman who oversaw the unification of Germany. He is believed to have said, "People who love sausage and respect the law should never watch either of them being made." Another version is, "Laws are like sausages. It's better not to see them being made."

The Industrial Revolution

The Industrial Revolution saw the production of sausage move from the butcher shops to the factory floor. Industrially produced sausages not only required fewer people, but these sausages could be transported farther distances thanks to the introduction of chemically produced preservatives.

The September 1868 edition of *The Grocer* describes how the Hillier sausage factory worked. "Women of exceptional cleanliness and men clothed in blouses of spotless white" used steam-powered machines to churn out 215,000 pounds of sausages, which were distributed by rail in 20-pound packages costing 9 pence each.

While factories staffed by exceptionally clean women and spotlessly dressed men churned out masses of sausages, the kitchen itself was reorganized by the culinary great, Georges Auguste Escoffier.

This great chef, restaurateur, and culinary writer revolutionized a cooking system for professional kitchens called the *brigade de cuisine*, or kitchen brigade organization. To this day, most professional kitchens continue to operate under Escoffier's system. Under this system, sausages fell to the chef called the *garde manger*, who was in charge of all the charcuterie as well as the salads, cold cuts, and all types of food preservation. Today, garde mangers continue to make sausages in restaurants.

Factories continued to make sausages as well. But through all this change, small butchers and artisan sausage makers have survived, and the fine tradition continues.

Globally Infused Sausages

Starting in the 1990s, some top chefs in New York and Los Angeles began combining diverse culinary traditions into single dishes. For example, chefs added Asian spices such as ginger and cardamom to French fois gras and stuffed Italian raviolis with bok choy and topped them with a Thai peanut sauce. Over the last two decades, this trend, called global fusion, has spread.

Both simple sandwich shops and five-star restaurants have adopted this practice. It's not unheard of to find an Asian-spiced fois gras combined with a savory English scone made with African spices or an Italian panna cotta made with Mexican mangoes.

Sausage making has been affected by this trend as well. Instead of making a simple Polish kielbasa, some chefs combine their recipes with Mexican chorizo, creating a Mexican-Polish hybrid sausage. Kielrizo, anyone?

Chef Daniel Boulud is one of the most famous chefs making global fusion sausages. He offers a dozen different sausages on the menu at his DBGB restaurant in New York City, including a veal bratwurst, a "tunisienne" merguez sausage made of lamb and mint, and an "espagnole," or French-styled Spanish sausage made with basil oil (which is never an ingredient in Spanish chorizo). On a much smaller scale, Yuppie

Hill Poultry, a Burlington, Wisconsin, chicken farmer and artisan sausage maker, laces ginger into traditional breakfast sausage patties.

Whether it's sausage or fois gras, raviolis or fried rice, fusion cuisine starts with a chef's individual preferences and the random thought, "I wonder how it would taste if I combined this ingredient with that spice." Throughout the chapters of this book, you'll find suggestions for global fusion adaptations of traditional recipes.

As you become a more adept sausage maker, you'll be able to tweak sausage recipes to your specific desires—adding more garlic to the hot Italian sausage recipe, for example—and even go so far as to try your own global fusions. If you like coffee, mix it into your sausages. A huge lemongrass fan? Go ahead and add it to your sausages. You can make a bratwurst using ground chicken meat, studding it with Italian herbs, if you so desire. Basically, the sky's the limit to the kind of sausages you can create.

The Least You Need to Know

- Industrial sausages appeal to the largest demographic possible at the lowest cost possible. They often contain additives and chemicals.
- Artisan sausages are made of the highest-quality ingredients the sausage maker can find, including whole pork butt or pork shoulder.
- The first sausages were made thousands of years ago, using chopped meat combined with local spices and stuffed into intestines or stomachs.
- Globally infused sausages combine two or more culinary traditions in a single sausage; such fusion sausages are limited only by a chef's imagination.

Sausage Making Supplies and Equipment

In This Chapter

- A sampler platter of sausage meats
- The importance of choosing a good source for your meats
- Spices for flavoring your links
- How to choose the right casings
- Sausage making equipment and tools

There's an art to shopping for meats, and in this chapter we give you a chef's-eye view of choosing the right cuts for your sausages. In addition, we introduce you to the spices you need to add to your shopping list and give you some tips for finding the best casings.

Finally, we take a tour of your kitchen to see if it's equipped with the necessary appliances and tools. Although you don't need any specialized equipment to make homemade sausage, some handy gadgets make the process a whole lot easier.

An Overview of Sausage Meats

You can make sausage with just about any edible protein. Grind up anything from crab to venison, add some spices, form it into patties or links, and voilà, you have yourself some homemade sausage. But, by and large, traditional, artisanal sausages are made with pork.

Pork Sausages

Pork takes the starring role in most sausage recipes. Sometimes sausage makers combine pork with beef, but it's usually the solo star of the sausage show. That's because pork boasts the best fat for sausage making. To quote famed Cajun chef and restaurateur Emeril Lagasse, "Pork fat rules!" Its delicious richness envelops spices and salt, delivering them expertly to your tongue. In fact, in traditional French cooking, pork fat is sometimes wrapped around poultry meats to add moistness and flavor. That's the same reason cooks wrap bacon around everything from scallops to potatoes—for the fat and flavor.

Although commercial sausage makers use various cuts of pork and pork fat—including unmentionable cuts of meat—artisan sausage makers are much more selective.

Most recipes for pork sausage call for *pork butt* or pork shoulder meat. Pork butt and pork shoulder actually refer to the same part of the pig, and it isn't actually the butt, but rather the top part of the pork shoulder, or hip area, of a pig leg.

DEFINITION

Pork butt, sometimes also called "Boston butt," is the top part of a whole pork shoulder. It's distinct from a shoulder roast or "pork picnic," which is the lower portion of shoulder meat, below the joint and above the shank (another name for pork leg) that contains fat, connective tissue, and bones.

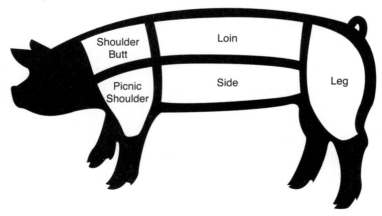

The pork picnic is located immediately below the pork shoulder or the shoulder butt.
(Designed by Bec Loss)

For the purposes of making sausages, it doesn't matter whether you get pork butt or whole pork shoulder.

Whole shoulder, pork butt, and Boston butt can all be used in sausage recipes, and butchers often use the terms interchangeably, even though they don't refer to exactly the same cuts. If you ask your local butcher for pork shoulder and he tells you he's got some great pork butt, go ahead and buy it.

Most sausages, especially traditional ones such as brats, Italian sausages, and breakfast sausage, combine butt or shoulder meat with extra pork fat, called *trimmings*. The trimmings usually come from the belly or the jowls.

 DEFINITION

Trimmings are the extra fat taken from all over the pig. These often include little bits of meat that would otherwise go to waste.

Shoulder or butt meat contains about 15 percent fat, making it a marbled cut of meat. It's a good cut to roast for barbecue pulled pork and ideal for sausage making. When you bite into a juicy sausage, it's the fat in the sausage that makes it so juicy, not the water content.

Most pork sausage recipes call for between 90 percent pork butt and 10 percent extra fat and 80 percent pork butt and 20 percent extra fat. By the time you're a proficient sausage maker, you'll know the ratio your taste buds and your arteries prefer.

Some recipes also call for other cuts of pork, like jowls or cheeks, and you can even throw these cuts into traditional recipes that call for pork butt. Jowl cuts aren't as visually appealing as whole cuts, but they are high-quality meat.

Beef Sausages

The second most commonly used meat in sausage making is beef. Baloney and hot dogs are made with beef, of course, as are many European sausages, particularly those from Eastern Europe, Germany, and Austria. The fat and meat ratio for making beef sausages is similar to that in pork sausages, but the spices and flavorings are different. Beef fat has a stronger, more distinct flavor than pork, and so requires different spices than those used to enhance the more neutral flavors of pork. Many sausage recipes that use beef call for beef chuck or shoulder meat. This meat comes from the neck and shoulder area of a cow. It's a flavorful and economical part of the animal.

Some sausage recipes use veal instead of beef. Veal, or the meat from a young calf, is more tender and mild in flavor than beef, and it's used in several German sausage recipes. Recipes calling for veal typically use similar fat and meat ratios as those in beef or pork recipes.

Lamb and Mutton Sausages

Lamb and mutton have been used in sausage making for centuries, especially in more mountainous regions where such animals are common.

Lamb is milder in flavor than mutton. Spring lamb, or young lamb, is even more delicately flavored. Mutton is a strongly flavored meat and is more of an acquired taste, especially in North America.

CHEF'S CHOICE

Some specialized recipes call for goat meat, which is also definitely an acquired taste. Even though goat meat is becoming more popular, it's far more difficult to obtain than lamb and mutton.

Sausages made with mutton and lamb use a ratio of 80 to 90 percent meat to 10 to 20 percent fat, but many sausage makers replace some of the sheep fat with pork fat to tone down the flavor.

Game Meats

Pork, beef, and lamb aren't the only sausage meat game in town. Game—*venison*, elk, buffalo, rabbit, and wild boar—can also be ground into sausages.

DEFINITION

Venison typically refers to deer meat or antelope meat, but technically it refers to the edible flesh of a game animal. Nonetheless, most recipes that call for venison want you to use deer meat.

Sausages made from game meats are leaner than pork, beef, and lamb sausages, and their flavor profiles are more interesting. They're "gamey," which means they have a stronger, more pronounced flavor. This gamey flavor comes from what the animals eat as well as their high levels of activity. As a result, game meat from a domestic deer farm, for example, will be less gamey than that from the 12-point wild buck your Uncle Chuck shot.

The gaminess of game meat is most pronounced in the fat of the meat. To cut down on the strong flavor, you should try to remove as much of the fat as possible when preparing game meat for sausage making. Chapter 13 walks you through the steps of doing this.

To replace the game fat you remove, most game sausage recipes call for pork fat, but the ratio of fat to meat is much leaner than that of pork or beef sausages.

Poultry and Seafood Sausages

You can make delicious sausages from duck, turkey, and chicken meats, as well as many different kinds of seafood. A region's favorite protein always ends up in the sausages, so you'll typically find seafood sausages in coastal areas and mutton sausages in more mountainous regions.

Poultry and seafood sausages have perhaps the leanest ratio of fat to meat because you add little or no extra fat to the meat. Since they're leaner, you will need to decrease the amount of spices. Chicken sausages are the mildest in flavor of all the poultry sausages; both turkey and duck sausages are richer in taste. Poultry sausages are often combined with vegetables and/or fruits for a richer, bolder taste.

Vegetarian Sausages

Traditionally, vegetarian cultures such as India don't have a sausage making heritage. However, you can make vegetarian sausages at home using beans, tofu, mushrooms, rice, and other hearty protein substitutes for meat. Mix these proteins with milk or egg whites, and there aren't any vegetarian casings. However, you can form "links" through other techniques, which are discussed in Chapter 12.

Rice also takes on a starring role in some Asian sausages. Rice sausages are mostly rice with a little protein thrown in to bind them together.

You can combine other ingredients, such as fruit, cheese, ham, and green onions in sausages. These are never the main ingredients, and they're typically added just before the sausage is linked or formed into patties. Because these ingredients aren't ground in with the meats and spices, they're considered *garnish*.

DEFINITION

Garnish refers to the extra ingredients mixed into the ground combination of meat, salt, and spices. When the sausage is linked, the garnish is studded throughout the sausages as nonground components.

Selecting Your Meat Purveyor

The four primary sources of sausage meat are as follows:

- Supermarkets
- Specialty grocery stores such as Whole Foods, gourmet markets, and food cooperatives
- Butcher shops
- Direct from farmers

You can also buy your meat from online meat purveyors, but most of these, with the exception of some steak companies, sell only prepared meat. It's difficult to ship a product that must remain refrigerated or frozen at a specific temperature. Some farmers ship their meat directly to consumers.

THE GRIND

As a general rule, don't buy meat that has to be delivered via a shipping service. Meat can only be safely frozen twice. If you buy it fresh at the grocery store, you can freeze it, use it, and then refreeze it again. If you buy it already frozen, you've already used up one of your freezing opportunities. (For more on handling meat safely, see Chapter 3.) In addition, meat can be quite expensive to ship.

Whether you buy your meat from a large grocery store, a specialty grocer, or a butcher, note the store's conditions. In particular, make sure it meets the following criteria:

- It's clean.
- They sell most of their meats before the sell-by date on the package.
- The staff is knowledgeable about various cuts of meat.

The most important criteria for choosing a source for your meat is that it has a healthy turnover rate for its meat. If the store is consistently restocking its meats, that's a good sign. In addition, be sure to look at the labels for the "use by," "sell by," or "packaged on" dates. The fresher the meat is, the better. Stockers generally put the oldest meat up front and the freshest meat in back. Don't hesitate to reach to the back of the stack to find the freshest cut.

Also, take time to get to know your meat seller or butcher. Whether you buy your meat from a large grocery chain or your corner butcher shop, talk to the staff who cuts the meat. The more face time you have with the people who handle the hog, the more knowledgeable you become.

One advantage to shopping in a small, well-maintained butcher shop over a large chain grocery is the intimate relationship you can develop with your purveyor. Chances are the guy behind the counter is the owner, and he has a stake in how happy you are with your steak. People who own or work in butcher shops tend to have a real passion for meat, and they're going to want to help you because they really care about their products.

PRIME CUT

A surprisingly good source for quality meats is chain food giant Costco. It has a fantastic selection of meat, poultry, and seafood items. Additionally, the meat is typically very fresh because of the chain's high turnover rate.

To find a local meat farmer, go to www.LocalHarvest.com and enter your zip code. You can also contact farmers through your state's farm organizations, such as the Wisconsin Pork Producers Association. Many *Community Supported Agriculture* (*CSA*) cooperatives also offer meat shares along with their vegetables. And don't forget farmers' markets!

DEFINITION

Community Supported Agriculture (CSA) is a food production and distribution system in which consumers purchase shares of food directly from the farmer before the growing season starts. Then, during the season, the farmer delivers your share each week. CSA helps the farmer because it allows him or her to purchase seeds, manure, and so on before making any profit, and it helps consumers, who get first pick of the farmer's crops.

Many farmers who specialize in selling meat locally also have websites, which tell you if, how, and where they ship meats. Keep in mind, however, that if you shop online, you can't see or touch the meat before you buy. A well-designed website doesn't guarantee that the store or farmer will have the best or the freshest meats.

Ingredients to Enhance Sausage Flavor

After meat, the most important sausage ingredients are salt and spices. While many sausage making traditions use the same meats and often prepare them using very similar methods, each tradition has its own salt and spice profiles.

Salt

If you look at the salt selection at a gourmet grocery store, you'll find table salt, sea salt, kosher salt, and even Himalayan salt blocks—not to mention fine ground salt, rough ground salt, and salt mixed with spices. Though the varied salts can be especially important when cooking, there's really only one type of salt you need to know about for making sausages: kosher or kosher-style salt.

Kosher salt comes in rough granules or larger flakes, which take a bit longer to break down than finely ground salts. Because sausage making is a long process, the flakes have time to break down slowly, which enhances the flavor.

In addition, kosher salt, unlike table salt, doesn't contain additives. Most table salt has been iodized, and the iodine can adversely affect the flavor of your sausage.

Sea salt, which is salt harvested from seawater, is great for cooking. However, it's also more expensive than kosher salt and contains some trace minerals from the seawater. Although minerals impart great flavors to cooked dishes, they're not needed when making sausages.

Spices

You can find most sausage spices at your local grocery store. Some basic spices to keep in your pantry include the following:

- Black pepper
- White pepper
- Garlic (powdered, granulated, or fresh)

- Onion (powdered, granulated, or fresh)
- Ground dry mustard
- Italian herbs, such as oregano and basil

You can get many of these ingredients from your local grocer, but you can also find some great spices from spice specialty shops like Penzeys and The Spice House, which have online stores, as well as brick-and-mortar stores in some areas of the country.

THE GRIND

The fresher the spices, the better the sausage. If you add stale spices to your sausage, you might as well just throw in some sawdust, too.

Ground spices last about two years before they lose their flavor. Whole spices can last up to four years. Put your spices in an airtight container and store them in a dark place.

How can you tell whether your spices should be tossed? Open the jar and sniff. If you open a jar of basil and it smells like basil, then it's good to use. If you don't smell anything or just a faint whiff, throw it out. The basic rule is if you can smell it—and we mean *really* smell it—you can use it.

Sausage Casings

In order to make linked sausages, you need casings to stuff the meat and spices into. The average grocery store doesn't carry sausage casings. You can buy them at hunting and outdoors equipment stores, but they typically stock only dry-packed casings, which can be difficult to work with. Your best bet for buying sausage casings locally is to go to an ethnic market, meat supplier, or butcher.

The following three types of casings are generally available:

- Natural (direct from the animal)
- Collagen (made from natural substances)
- Synthetic

Natural casings come from the intestines of cows, sheep, or hogs. Beef casings are large and are used for baloney-sized sausages. Sheep casings are used for breakfast links. Hog casings are used for most fresh and smoked sausages. Natural casings have the best mouthfeel of all the casings, are easy to bite through, and have a satisfying snap when bitten.

Collagen casings are made from collagen, which comes from the skins of animals. They are made from natural materials, but they are manufactured. Because they are manufactured, each casing is perfectly uniform and consistent, as opposed to natural casings with their natural imperfections. Collagen casings are also shelf stable, whereas natural casings have a limited shelf life. Collagen casings are easy to use, and in fact, they take no preparation to use, whereas natural casings do require a little more work. For more on working with casings, see Chapter 4.

Though collagen casings are easier to use than natural casings, they don't taste as good as natural casings. The mouthfeel of collagen casings is almost gummy, and you have to really chomp down on them to get to the delicious sausage filling.

Synthetic casings aren't edible and must be removed before the sausage is served. Sausage makers typically use them for summer sausage, liver sausage, and salami.

A local butcher can supply you with natural casings. You can order collagen and synthetic casings online from specialty sausage websites and even well-known websites such as Amazon.com.

Equipping Your Kitchen

The basic equipment for sausage making may already be in your kitchen. Here's what you'll need:

- Boning knife
- French knife
- Steel for honing knives
- Two large cutting boards
- Measuring spoons and cups
- Kitchen scale
- Bowls

- Industrial-sized pans
- Meat grinder
- Meat thermometer

A boning knife is a knife used to remove bones from raw meat. It has a thin, flexible blade that can curve around the bone to minimize waste. A French knife, also referred to as a French chef's knife or simply a chef's knife, is a thick, strong knife used to cut boneless meat into cubes. It can also be used to chop vegetables.

You will only need to use a boning knife to remove the actual bone; if you buy boneless meat, you can leave this knife in the drawer. The French knife will do everything else you need with sausages.

Make sure your knives are sharp. More accidents in the kitchen happen with dull knives than sharp knives. A dull knife is more likely to slip and cut you than a sharpened knife that can actually cut through food.

To maintain your knives' blades, use a *steel* to hone the blades every time you use them. (See Chapter 3 for details on using a steel.)

DEFINITION

A **steel** is a round metal rod with a handle used to hone the knife blade or "true the edge." It doesn't sharpen the blade; it only maintains the blade.

You should also have one or two large cutting boards on hand. Plastic boards are the easiest to sanitize, while wood and bamboo boards can warp or crack from high-temperature water. Ideally, you should have one cutting board for raw meat and a second board for poultry to minimize potential cross contamination. Try color-coding your boards: red for meat, yellow or white for poultry, and green for produce.

You'll also need measuring spoons and/or a kitchen scale to measure salt and spices. A kitchen scale is always more accurate than filling a measuring cup or spoon, but each recipe in this book includes both the weight and measurement equivalents for salt and spices.

To mix and grind the meat and spices, you need 4-quart bowls. An even better alternative to bowls is to use hotel pans, which are large, flat-bottomed, rectangle-shaped pans that come in standardized sizes ranging from full, half, third, and so on. They are used for prep work, buffet service, and storage in commercial kitchens. A half-sized hotel pan is perfect for making a 10-pound batch of sausages.

> **PRIME CUT**
>
> Sausage making requires a lot of setup and work, no matter what size batch you make. It usually isn't worth making batches any smaller than 5 or 10 pounds at a time.

You can find hotel pans at commercial kitchen supply stores. Most kitchen supply stores sell their wares to the public, and you can find all sorts of kitchen gadgets and goodies at these stores that can't be found elsewhere.

Meat Grinder

Beyond the basic equipment, you'll need a meat grinder. The results from grinding your own meat are much better than buying it preground at the store. Only use preground meat if you're in a hurry. If you grind your own meat, you have control over the fat content and more control over the texture and taste.

If you really get into sausage making, you'll likely want to purchase a separate, stand-alone meat grinder. These babies start at about $85, and they can go up to $1,000. They're great for grinding meat, but for most home chefs, they're an unnecessary expense.

For starters, it's perfectly acceptable to buy a meat grinding attachment for your mixer. A standard meat grinding attachment costs about $45. Attached grinders are slower and less efficient than stand-alone meat grinders, but they get the job done.

You can also use a hand grinder. You can buy them new or used for anywhere from $25 to $100. Whether you inherit one, pick one up secondhand, or buy one brand new, hand grinders are much, much slower than a stand-alone grinder or a mixing bowl attachment but they do a good job of grinding the meat.

You can't always tell if a sausage is completely cooked just by looking at it. Therefore, a meat thermometer is a good piece of equipment to have on hand when you are cooking sausages and other meats. It's especially important when making smoked sausages.

If this is all the equipment you have, then you're ready to make bulk sausages. If you're planning to make linked sausages, you will also need a sausage stuffer.

THE GRIND

Avoid using mixing bowl sausage stuffing attachments. You're more likely to get air pockets using this type of stuffer. Plus, they can be very frustrating to work with.

There are two kinds of sausage stuffing appliances: lever-powered and gear-driven. Both work well. A lever-powered stuffer, usually sized with a 3-pound capacity maximum, can be operated by one person. A gear-driven stuffer, typically 5-pound capacity or more, is best operated by two people.

Although manufacturers say that you can stuff 3 pounds of meat into a lever-powered stuffer, we recommend using only half that amount. Any more than that and the lever is hard to push down. To be on the safe side and make your job easier, don't push the capacity to the limit on any stuffer.

A good stuffer or extruder starts at about $70 to $100, but they can go as high as $2,000. You only need an inexpensive stuffer, but it's an essential piece of equipment for making brats and Polish and Italian sausages. You can find them online, and you can also purchase them at outdoor/hunting and camping supply stores.

Vacuum Sealer

One other piece of equipment you might want to purchase is a vacuum packer or sealer. It allows you to freeze large batches of sausages without fear of them succumbing to freezer burn. While you can freeze your sausages in containers or plastic baggies, they are more likely to incur freezer burn if you don't vacuum seal them first. If you plan on making large batches of sausages, the vacuum sealer will ensure that when you freeze them, they stay fresh. They can be found at department stores, culinary equipment stores, and even outdoor equipment stores. Expect to pay from $50 to $200 for the device and $10 for a set of plastic bags.

The Least You Need to Know

- Pork butt or pork shoulder is the main ingredient for most of the sausages you'll want to make.
- Cleanliness, turnover, and knowledge of staff are the main things you look for in a meat purveyor.

- To tell if your spices are fresh enough to make sausages, simply sniff.
- You will need knives, cutting boards, and large bowls to make sausages.
- A meat grinder or grinding attachment and a sausage stuffer are essential equipment for making linked sausages.

Food and Kitchen Safety

In This Chapter

- Kitchen sanitation procedures
- Safely handling raw meat
- The importance of preparation
- Minimizing risk of injury with knives and meat grinders
- Packaging, storing, and transporting your sausages

Most of us understand the importance of proper sanitation when handling food. We also recognize the value in following safety procedures when using potentially dangerous kitchen instruments. Nonetheless, sometimes we aren't as careful as we should be.

Kitchen safety is especially important when you're dealing with raw meat, and it's also very important when you're using knives and grinders. Because sausage making involves both raw meat and dangerous equipment, the possibilities for erring increase exponentially, and the stakes for mistakes grow even higher.

Fortunately, basic sanitation and safety practices prevent most accidents and are easy to follow. This chapter highlights the importance of safety and sanitation, and it also shows you how to properly handle your meat and your prepared sausages. Finally, it details how to package, store, and transport your sausages safely.

The Importance of Proper Sanitation

All sorts of harmful bacteria can be found in improperly handled food products. In recent years in the United States alone, there have been numerous recalls of everything from spinach to ground beef to fish sticks. Every time someone handling food fails to wash his hands or uses unclean utensils, dishes, or equipment, he puts countless people at risk for outbreaks of serious illnesses and even death.

Proper kitchen sanitation is even more important when you're handling raw or uncooked foods, which can be a bacterium's idea of party central. Outbreaks of salmonella, campylobacter, listeria, and e. coli bacteria can often be traced to improper cleaning and/or handling of raw or uncooked food items.

THE GRIND

Salmonella, campylobacter, listeria, and e. coli (esterichia coli) are all potentially deadly types of bacteria, and that is why it is utterly important to follow proper sanitation techniques.

Fortunately, you can take simple steps to minimize the likelihood of contamination. The three most important ways to minimize contamination are as follows:

- Wash your hands with soap and water regularly, particularly after handling raw meat.
- Clean all kitchen surfaces regularly.
- Use only very fresh meat.

The following sections explore these basic concepts in more detail.

Keep Your Hands Washed

Food safety starts with clean hands and a clean kitchen. Simply put: if you wash your hands, they won't have the harmful bacteria on them. If your hands don't have bacteria on them, you won't transfer it to your refrigerator door, your face, or other foods.

To give you an idea of just how easy it is for a little bit of bacteria to cause infection, a friend of ours suffered food poisoning simply because, while handling raw meat, she wiped the back of her hand on her face. It's that easy to make yourself sick. But if you remember to wash your hands, it's also that easy to prevent illness.

If you touch raw meat, stop. Before you do anything else, wash your hands. Use hot water and soap, and scrub them for at least 15 seconds (about how long it takes you to sing the first stanza of "Happy Birthday"). Dry your hands on a clean towel, then continue with whatever else you need to do.

PRIME CUT

If you wear gloves while handling raw meat, make sure you remove them after you handle meat and before you touch any clean surfaces. After you touch raw meat, throw out your gloves *and* wash and dry your hands before you do anything else.

Another important tip is to make sure the gloves are food grade. You can buy these kinds of gloves in bulk from kitchen supply stores, and you can also find them online and in supermarkets. We recommend using latex-free gloves in case you share your sausage with anyone who has a latex allergy.

Other Cleanliness Rules to Live By

If you can live with the flashbacks to your high school cafeteria, it's also a good idea to wear a hair net. Or if you prefer, don your favorite team's baseball cap. The main purpose of a hair net or hat is to restrain your hair. If you have long hair, pull it back into a ponytail and then put on a hat or hair net.

Much like gloves, head coverings can be quite harmful when used improperly. Never remove hats, even if just to adjust them, in the kitchen. If you do this, you have a very good chance of dropping some hairs into your food. One tip that Jeff practices: if he needs to reposition his hat to cover some loose hair, he always steps into the bathroom first. There, he washes his hands, takes care of his hat, and then washes his hands again before returning to the kitchen.

Another thing to remember is to remove your rings before you start making sausage. That way, they won't be contaminated by the meat, and you also won't have to worry about them getting caught on anything in the kitchen.

If you have long fingernails, keep a nailbrush next to your kitchen sink to scrub out any meat particles that get trapped. And, of course, remember to wash that brush with hot water, soap, and bleach, too.

Wear comfortable, closed-toe shoes such as sneakers when making sausages. If your feet hurt, then your back might start aching, and if your feet and your back aren't happy, then chances are you'll start slouching or using bad posture, which will further aggravate everything and make you careless while using sharp tools. It's important to keep your feet fully covered because you don't want any knives that fall to accidentally cut your feet.

Keep Your Kitchen Clean

Your countertops don't necessarily need to be clean enough to "eat off of" on a daily basis, but when working with sausage, it's a good idea to wash down the whole counter. This is because there's a good chance you'll spill some of the meat somewhere along the way. If anything falls to the floor, onto a dirty counter, or on anything else that is only questionably clean, toss it. The old stand-by "When in doubt, throw it out," applies to sausage making. It simply isn't worth the risk of sending someone to the hospital.

After you prepare raw meat on your counters, you should not only wash them down with soap and water, but you should also wipe them with a mixture of 1 part bleach to 10 parts water. An easy way to do this is to keep a spray bottle of bleach water on hand. You can also use the spray bottle to rinse off your cutting boards.

It doesn't matter whether your cutting boards are wood, bamboo, or plastic. One kind isn't necessarily more sanitary than the others. The thing with wood and bamboo, however, is, if your knives nick them, those little nicks tend to naturally seal up, whereas plastic boards get grooves in them that never disappear.

Some people like to keep one or two cutting boards reserved just for cutting meat, but that can lead to carelessness. The main thing is to clean your cutting board after you use it. If you chopped meat on your board, then you also need to clean it (and then the sink) with your bleach mixture. Simply rinse and soap up your cutting board, spray it with bleach water, then rinse it again and dry it.

After you clean your kitchen and equipment, use clean towels, aprons, and sponges. You don't want your dirty towels or sponges to recontaminate an area as you "clean" it.

PRIME CUT

Two simple methods to clean your sponges are to put them through the dishwasher or to microwave them on high for 1 minute.

After you've cleaned your kitchen but before you remove your meat from the fridge, take some time to prepare. Take out all the equipment you'll need for each step and set it up before you get started. The French call this concept *mis-en-place*, which can be loosely translated as "get your stuff together."

DEFINITION

Mis-en-place is a French term that means "everything in its place." Almost every French cooking lesson starts with a mini lecture on the importance of readying everything—tools, ingredients, recipes—before you start making a dish.

If you have everything in place before you start, you won't have to take off your gloves, wash your hands, and then start rummaging around in your cupboards and drawers to look for that certain knife or box of salt. Having everything ready to go also saves you time and headaches and helps keep you safe.

Proper mis-en-place can also prevent strains and work-related injuries. If all your equipment, supplies, and ingredients are where you will most likely use them, you'll be less likely to strain a muscle by contorting yourself to reach an ingredient or tool.

Keep Meat Fresh

Now, here's the thing with raw meat: most bacteria start out on the surface. If you cook a steak, you kill the bacteria. But if you take that raw meat and grind it up, any minute amounts of bacteria that might have been on the surface of the meat— amounts that might not even be harmful—get mixed throughout the meat.

This, in and of itself, isn't a problem if you handle the meat properly. If you keep it at the right temperature for the right amount of time, that little bit of bacteria won't have a chance to grow before you have a chance to cook your sausages. However, if you leave your meat sitting out on the counter for an unsafe period of time, you're courting trouble.

The basic rule for raw meat, poultry, and seafood is that it should only be kept at room temperature for a total of 4 hours before cooking.

THE GRIND

Raw meat, poultry, and seafood should never be left outside of the refrigerator for more than 4 hours total. That includes transportation from the store to your house, and it includes chopping, grinding, stuffing, and so on. Follow this rule to keep from getting sick.

Let's detail the potential amount of time you have based on some estimated times for preparing sausage from scratch:

- 30 minutes shopping for meat

- 30 minutes deboning and cubing meat

- 30 minutes grinding meat

- 30 minutes stuffing sausage

- 30 minutes linking sausage

- 30 minutes packaging sausage

So far that comes to 3 hours, which leaves you with an hour fudge factor. The salt and spice mixes you add to your sausages extend this 4-hour safety window a bit by acting as preservatives, but it's important to minimize any unnecessary time that your meat goes unrefrigerated. That doesn't leave much time to let the meat sit on the counter. To minimize the amount of time your meat is at room temperature, put your meat back in the fridge after each and every step in the sausage making process.

It's also equally important to clean your counters, your equipment, and your hands after each step in the process. You cut up and cube your meat, put it in the refrigerator, and you clean up. You grind your meat, mix in the salt and spices, put it in the refrigerator, and you clean up. Prepare, then clean. Cook, then clean.

After you touch the meat with your hands, before you touch anything else, wash your hands. Every time. Make sure your dirty knives, cutting boards, and other used equipment don't come in contact with a clean counter or clean dishes. Be aware of where your used equipment is and what it's touching—bacteria can spread just as easily from dirty dishes or dirty sink surfaces as they can dirty hands.

THE GRIND

Make sure your dirty knives and cutting boards don't touch a clean counter or clean dishes. That's an easy way to spread a food-borne illness.

Using Equipment Safely

Before you get out your knives and your grinder, the first thing you want to do is to make sure there's nothing on the floor that you can trip on. That includes the family dog or cat that might be drawn to the kitchen by the delicious aromas they smell while you prepare your sausages.

The first lesson in knife safety, besides not running with them, is to keep them sharp. Dull knives cause more accidents than sharp knives. Ever have a knife slip off of a slippery tomato skin while you're trying to cut it? That only happens when the knife is dull, not sharp.

Have your knives professionally sharpened at least once a year. Some specialty kitchen and gourmet food stores offer this service. You should also hone your knives before each use with a steel. If you don't have a steel, you can sharpen your knives regularly on a home knife sharpener, but it's a poor substitute.

There is a bit of a knack to honing your knife on a steel. Follow these steps:

1. Hold the steel with your nondominant hand and the knife with your dominant hand. Plant the tip of the rod on a cutting board using your non-dominant hand to hold the handle. Your thumb should be up, with your palm facing inward.

2. While holding the steel firmly, use your dominant hand to run the blade against the steel at a 20° angle.

3. Start with the heel of the blade (the part nearest the handle) at the top of the steel and run the blade down and across the steel so the tip of your knife comes off near the bottom. Your stroke should be gentle and smooth.

4. Repeat this process on the other side of the blade.

5. Repeat 10 times on each side.

Honing takes some getting used to, but it's well worth the time to figure it out. If this process still seems a little unclear to you, you can hop onto the Internet and watch the following instructional video on YouTube: www.youtube.com/watch?v=qcKoUO5JqYc. Or simply do a search for "how to steel a knife" and watch one of the many videos that demonstrate different techniques.

Grinder Safety

The main rule of thumb—at least if you want to keep your thumbs attached to your hands—is to never, ever, ever reach down into the grinder while it's running. This same rule applies to knives, wooden spoons, and, of course, your precious fingers.

Always turn off the grinder and unplug it (so that it won't get accidentally turned on via a power surge or by a naïve co–sausage maker).

It's equally important to read those directions that come with the grinder. Technical manuals are sometimes a boring read, but it's very important to understand the equipment you're using.

Clean your grinder before and after you use it. If you haven't made sausages for a while, your grinder may have gotten dusty, and you really don't want dust particles flavoring your sausage. Even if your grinder is new, clean it before you use it to wash off the chemicals and/or oils that may have touched it during the manufacturing process.

Follow the same cleaning habits for your stuffer. However, when you clean your stuffer, don't clean the concealed mechanical area or the plunger shaft that comes out of each side. Both of these parts are coated with grease that help the stuffer run smoothly.

Don't touch any portion of the shaft of the stuffer above the plunger. This area, which is often covered by a plate, has machine grease on it, and you don't want this grease contaminating your sausages.
(Photo by Kyle Edwards)

Needless to say, you don't want machine grease getting mixed into your sausage so the basic rule is, even though you can see this area, don't stick your fingers on it! Secondly, always keep protective plates in place. When you clean them, clean their surfaces, never their interior.

Refrigerating and Freezing Your Sausages

If you plan to cook and eat your freshly prepared sausages right away, you don't need to freeze them. Simply put them in a tightly sealed container and store them in the fridge for up to 3 days.

If you don't plan to consume your sausages within 3 days, you should freeze them. Even if you eat some of your sausages soon after making them, you'll probably have some leftover sausages to freeze. After all, making sausage is such a labor-intensive process it's best to make larger batches and freeze part of them.

The main problem with freezing sausages is the potential for *freezer burn*. Freezer burn can only occur when there is a pocket of air between your meat and the surrounding packaging. That pocket of air allows frost to form, which in turn "burns" the food. To prevent freezer burn, wrap the sausages tightly in plastic wrap, put them in another container or cover them with foil, and then seal them in a bag. That process of wrapping, then foiling, then wrapping again, minimizes your chances of having your sausages suffer the burn.

DEFINITION

Freezer burn is when air trapped inside or surrounding a frozen container destroys the meat inside. You can prevent freezer burn by keeping your meat tightly sealed.

By far the best way to prevent freezer burn, particularly for long-term freezing, is to seal your sausages using a vacuum packer. Vacuum packers, also called food sealers, suck out the excess air and seal the bags shut, thereby eliminating the possibility of freezer burn.

Vacuum sealers are also great for preparing any other food for the freezer, including soups, casseroles, and sauces. They're also great for preserving fresh fruits and veggies that you buy in season and plan to freeze.

Smoked and cured sausages can be refrigerated or frozen, and some are even shelf-stable. See Chapter 14 for details on storing smoked and cured sausage.

Transporting Sausages Safely

The easiest and safest way to transport sausage is to freeze it first, especially if you're transporting the sausage 2 or more days after you've made it. If you plan to transport your sausage to another site to prepare it, first boil and chill the sausage at home, then finish cooking it (grilling, roasting, etc.) on site.

Either way, it is best to transport the sausage in well-sealed containers that are put in a cooler and packed with ice.

You can also cook sausage completely, chill it, and then transport in an ovenproof dish. When you're ready to eat it, simply reheat the sausage in an oven. Chapter 17 covers more techniques for cooking, heating, and reheating sausages.

The Least You Need to Know

- Wash your hands immediately before and after you touch raw meat and equipment used to process the meat.
- Use a 1 part bleach to 10 parts water mixture to wipe down your counters and clean your equipment.
- Raw meat, poultry, and seafood can only be kept at room temperature for a maximum of 4 hours.
- Always use sharp knives and cleaned equipment.
- To prevent freezer burn, package it tightly or vacuum seal it.

Link It Up: Sausage Making Techniques

In This Chapter

- Prepping meat and spices
- Grinding and mixing meat
- Stuffing casings
- Linking sausages

Making sausages is an art form, but you still need to follow certain steps to ensure a safe, quality product. You start by finding out how to prep your meat for grinding. When you've got a handle on how to grind meat and mix in spices and garnishes, you're ready to make bulk sausage. And after becoming acquainted with the process of stuffing casings and linking them into individual sausages, you're on your way to sausage nirvana.

You can use the techniques in this chapter for making the recipes in this book or any other sausage recipes you find.

Preparing Your Meat and Spices

With a clean work area and supply of meat and other ingredients in hand, you're ready to begin making sausages. If you bought boneless meat, you need to cube the meat before grinding it; however, if you bought meat with a bone or bones in it, you will first need to remove the bone(s).

Removing the Meat from the Bone

To remove the meat from the bone, locate the bone with one hand. With your other hand, use a sharp boning knife to cut from the surface directly through the meat to the bone without actually digging into the bone.

Carve along the bone, cutting the meat away from the bone and peeling it back to one side.

To minimize the amount of meat you leave on the bone, let the knife blade glide through the meat as you remove it from the bone. Don't worry if a few chunks of meat remain with the bone; you can go back to remove them after cutting off the rest of the meat. You probably won't remove all of the meat from the bone on your first try, so just do your best.

> **PRIME CUT**
>
> Don't worry if you don't remove all of the meat from the bone. Bones with little bits of meat attached to them are great for making soup stocks. After you've finished making sausage, you can throw the bones in a pot with water and vegetables to make a delicious soup stock (see the White Pork Stock recipe in Chapter 15), or you can freeze the bones to make the stock later.

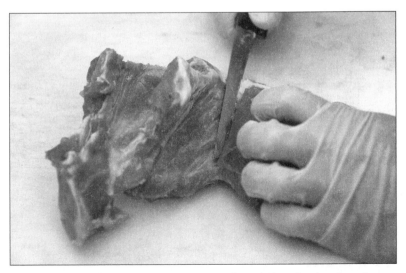

Hold the meat with one hand, hold your knife with the other hand, and carve along the bone, peeling back the meat as you cut it away from the bone.
(Photo by Kyle Edwards)

Cubing Your Meat

After you remove the bone from the meat (or if you purchased boneless meat), you need to cube the meat before you stick it in the grinder. The size of your cubes depends on the type of grinder you use. If you have an industrial-sized grinder—a stand-alone grinder that isn't attached to a kitchen mixer—you can cut the meat into 1½-inch cubes.

If your grinder doesn't have that kind of horsepower, make your cubes no larger than ¾ inch in size.

Use your French knife to cube the meat. The cubes don't have to be pretty or perfectly square since you're going to grind them up. They just need to be about the same size, and they should easily fit into the mouth of your grinder.

Holding Your Knives

Besides keeping your knives sharp and honed (see Chapter 3 for details), it's important to hold your knife correctly. Always grasp your knife with the handle between your thumb and four fingers. The hilt of the blade should be between your index finger and middle finger. Don't put your index finger on top of the blade to guide it. Instead, place your finger against the side of the blade (see the following figure). Holding the knife this way gives you much more control than just gripping the knife.

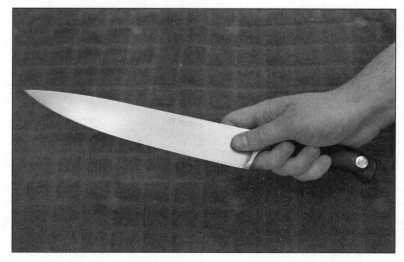

Grasp the knife between your index finger and your thumb, wrapping your other three fingers around the hilt of the knife.
(Photo by Kyle Edwards)

Use your other hand to firmly grasp the meat, but curl your fingers and thumb under so that you don't nip the ends of your finger when you slice through the meat. You can use a knife guard to protect your fingers, but it's not necessary if you're careful.

THE GRIND

Always lay your knives down with the blade facing to the side. Never, ever put them down with the blades facing up—that's a serious accident waiting to happen. Many kitchen knife accidents occur because people improperly set aside the knife after use, not during the actual cutting process.

While you're deboning the meat, you might come across tough pieces of cartilage and/or bone shards. You can distinguish cartilage and bone shards from the meat because they are much harder to cut. Remove them and throw them out. You also might come across some stringy fat or connective tissue—you can identify this because it is slimier than the rest of the meat. Again, cut this away and discard it.

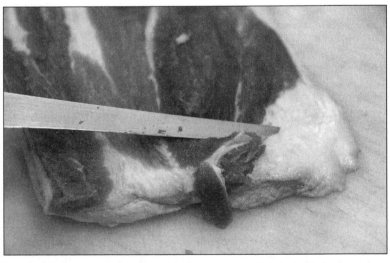

Notice how the cartilage stands out from the meat and the fat.
(Photo by Kyle Edwards)

Place the cubed meat in a large mixing bowl or hotel pan, cover it, and put it in the refrigerator before you clean up your kitchen and prepare to spice your meat.

Spicing It Up

It's time to measure out your spices and salt. We prefer weighing salt with a kitchen scale because it's more accurate than measuring spoons and cups, but you can use either.

CHEF'S CHOICE

If you substitute kosher salt with a finer grade of salt, you need to adjust the quantity if you're using measuring spoons. With a finer grade of salt, such as sea salt, more salt (and less air) fits into a measuring spoon. The recipes in this book use about 1 tablespoon kosher salt per 2 pounds meat. If you use table salt or fine ground sea salt and are measuring it out with a measuring spoon, use 2 teaspoons salt per 2 pounds meat.

Mix the spices and salt in a bowl. Remove the meat from the refrigerator and stir the salt and spices to coat the meat evenly. You can use a large wooden spoon or your clean hands to toss the spices and salt with the meat.

Although you can mix the spices and salt into the meat after you've ground it, you're better off mixing them in prior to grinding because they will be more thoroughly incorporated into your sausages.

Sometimes, though, you might want a spice or ingredient to stand out from the meat. In this case, don't mix it with the meat before you grind. For example, some Italian sausage recipes call for whole fennel seed to be mixed in after the meat is ground. In this case, the fennel seed is a garnish, meant to add a different texture and flavor to the sausage.

After you've combined the meat cubes with the salt and spices, put them in a covered container in the refrigerator. Clean up your kitchen before moving on to the next step.

THE GRIND

Always store your meat in the refrigerator and clean your kitchen between steps. This keeps the meat cold and your work area sanitary, which helps prevent the growth of harmful bacteria.

Grinding Your Meat

Chill your meat in the refrigerator or freezer for at least 30 minutes prior to grinding it. The colder your meat cubes are, the easier it is to grind them. Meat grinders produce friction, which in turn produces heat. Heat tends to melt the fat in meat a bit, which makes the cubes mushy. The mushier the cubes, the messier the grinding process.

You can also freeze your grinding attachment. Simply put it in the freezer for at least 60 minutes before you plan to use it. If you plan ahead, you can also stick it in the freezer overnight; it won't harm the machine at all.

Before you take your meat out of the refrigerator or freezer—and before you stick any attachments into the freezer—make sure that your grinder is clean. If it's been sitting for a while since you last made sausage, wipe it down. You don't want any dust particles getting in your sausage.

Setting Up Your Grinder

Although grinders vary in style and features, they all typically have three grinding plates, as follows:

- Fine plates have $\frac{1}{8}$-inch holes
- Medium plates have $\frac{1}{4}$-inch holes
- Coarse plates have $\frac{3}{8}$-inch holes

Most recipes call for a small or medium plate. If you're using a coarser grinding plate, you might want to grind the meat a second time. This will more likely be the case if you use an old-fashioned hand grinder because it will not be as consistent as a machine.

CHEF'S CHOICE

After you've been making sausages for a while, you'll know whether you prefer a finer or coarser grind for your sausages, and you can choose the plate and the number of grinds based on your preferences. That's one of the benefits of making your own sausage: you get to choose the grind you like, no matter what the recipe calls for!

Follow the instructions that come with your grinder to attach the appropriate plate to your grinder. Make sure everything is properly aligned and that nothing—including the plunger you use to push the meat through—is in the grinder. Turn it on. If everything is in good working order, begin grinding.

Putting Meat Into the Grinder

Start by pushing just a few cubes of meat through the grinder. Go slowly and methodically, and don't fill the grinder so that it's brimming with meat cubes. If you overstuff it, it will back up and make a mess.

Feed the meat slowly, using a plunger or a wooden spoon.
(Photo by Kyle Edwards)

If the meat backs up, you probably either put too much meat into the feeder or a piece of gristle or cartilage got stuck in the machine. Turn off the machine and unplug it. Remove the plate and check the blade of the grinder to see if any connective tissue or meat is blocking the flow. Remove whatever is causing the blockage, reassemble the grinder, plug the machine back in, and start grinding again.

Adding Spices and Sampling Your Sausage

If your recipe calls for mixing in any liquids and garnishes to the ground meat, use your hands or a tabletop mixer to combine the ingredients.

If you're making bulk sausage, you've just made your first batch of sausage. If you're making links, typically the next step is to stuff the sausages into a casing and link them. However, it's always a good idea to make a small test patty before calling the sausage done (if making bulk) or moving on to the next step (if making links).

Roll a dollop of sausage mixture—about the size of a half dollar—into a patty and fry it in a pan over medium heat. Taste it. If you like how it tastes, you're ready to stuff and link your sausages. If you're not satisfied with the flavors, adjust your seasonings, make another patty, cook it, and sample it. Repeat this process until you're satisfied with your test patty. You can't change the flavor profile of your sausage after it's linked, so it's best to tinker with the recipe now.

Keep in mind, however, that the seasonings and salt become more pronounced as your sausage sits in the refrigerator overnight. The flavors meld and come forward the longer your sausage sits.

The first time you make a sausage recipe, you might not want to adjust the seasonings from what the recipe dictates until you know the difference between how the sausage will taste at that test patty stage and after it's linked. After you've made sausages once or twice, you have a better sense of whether or not the recipe's seasoning and salt recommendations meet your preferences.

Congratulations! You just made your first batch of bulk sausage. If that's your end goal, put your finished product in containers, store them in the refrigerator or freezer, and clean up your kitchen.

Linking Your Sausage

Most people consider stuffing and linking to be the hardest parts of making sausage. The job is best done with two people—one person to crank the stuffer and the other to handle the sausage that's being linked. As you get more adept at making sausage, you'll be able to do it by yourself, but it's still easiest if you have a sausage buddy to assist.

Get Stuffing

Set up your stuffing machine on a counter or a table where you have some space to link your sausage. We recommend an area of at least 2 feet by 4 feet so you can work without feeling cramped. Make sure that the counter or table is clean.

If you're using a table that has a seam in the middle, cover the entire area with overlapping strips of plastic wrap to stop anything from leaking through. Then, drizzle a little bit of water on the surface so that the filled links will not stick to the counter or table. You can also use a spray bottle. If they stick, they have a tendency to tear or burst.

You will need about 2 feet of hog casings or 4 feet of sheep casings for each pound of sausage you make. When you're first starting, make sure you have extra casing because you may need it.

If you're using collagen casings, simply attach them to your stuffer. Natural casings, which taste a bit better, take a bit more prep work. If you use salt-packed casings that are vacuum packed—the kind available at many outdoors/hunting stores—first soak the casing in a large bowl of warm water. Each brand of vacuum-packed casings has its own set of directions; some require an overnight soaking, others don't.

If you purchased your casings from a butcher, they are preserved in a brine. Rinse off the brine before stuffing your meat into them. To do so, find an end to one casing and pull it out of the container. Take that end and gently rinse it in your sink. Next, spray water directly into the casing to fill it; it will expand like you're filling a water balloon, but the water will run through the casing unless it's knotted at the other end.

THE GRIND

If you don't properly rinse the casings, the leftover salt will adversely affect your sausages when you link and cook them.

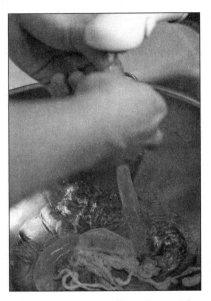

Rinse the salt out of the casings before stuffing them with your sausage mixture.
(Photo by Kyle Edwards)

As you thoroughly rinse the casing, remove any small knots or kinks in it. After you've rinsed off all the salt, put the casings in a bowl with a little water and set the bowl next to your stuffing station.

Use a damp cloth to moisten the end, or horn, of your sausage stuffer and glide one end of the casing onto it. Slowly slide the rest of the casing onto the horn until almost the entire length of casing is on the horn.

Slide the entire casing onto the horn of the sausage stuffer.
(Photo by Kyle Edwards)

Leave enough casing hanging off the end of the horn to tie a knot. Then, slowly, begin cranking the meat through.

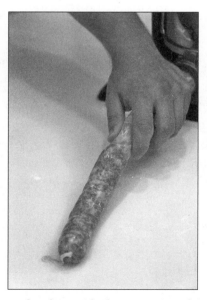

Use your thumb to guide the sausage into the casing.
(Photo by Kyle Edwards)

Hold on to the casing with your thumb at the horn to control the rate at which the meat fills the casing. If you hold it too tightly, you will overstuff the casing; if you hold it too loosely, the casing will be underfilled.

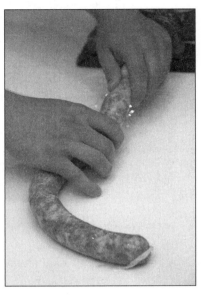

Crank the sausage stuffer at a speed that you're comfortable stuffing the sausage.
(Photo by Kyle Edwards)

As your sausage is being stuffed into the casing, coil it.
(Photo by Kyle Edwards)

Leave 4 to 6 inches of unstuffed casing at the very end of your sausage. This extra casing will get filled as you push the meat toward the end of the sausage during the linking process.

Leave enough casing to take up the extra sausage that gets pushed to the end as you link it.
(Photo by Kyle Edwards)

After you've stuffed your first link, check for any air pockets or bubbles. Where air pockets are present, the casing is transparent. Prick the pockets with the end of a sharp knife or a sewing needle to release the air and allow the meat to contact the casing.

It is easier when one person cranks the stuffer and the other person coils the sausage.
(Photo by Kyle Edwards)

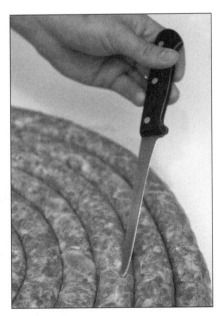

Air bubbles or pockets of air are easy to see because there isn't any meat behind the casing and is translucent. Use a knife or a needle to gently release the air in the bubble.
(Photo by Kyle Edwards)

You're now ready to link your sausage.

Linking It All Together

Linking can be the most challenging step in sausage making, but the more you do it, the easier it gets.

First, decide how long you want your links to be. If your brat bun is 6 inches long, your link should be just over 6 inches—about 6½ or 7 inches.

> **PRIME CUT**
>
> Unlike industrial sausages, which shrink drastically during the cooking process because of the high amount of fat and water that cooks out, your artisan sausages will be about the same size cooked as they are raw.

Measure your sausage using a ruler, tape measure, or even the kind of bun you plan to use to hold your sausage. If you use a bun, throw it away after you use it because it was in contact with raw meat.

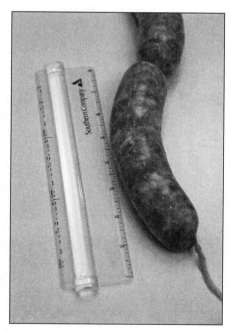

Until you know how to measure links with your hands, use a tape measure or a ruler to create links of consistent length.
(Photo by Kyle Edwards)

Pinch the sausage where you want to link it. Grab onto the end and twist it in one complete rotation. Measure again and pinch the sausage, but this time twist the link in the opposite direction to avoid untwisting the previous link.

Twist the sausage at least once or twice to create a link. Twist each link opposite of each other because otherwise, when you create one link, you are untwisting the previous link.
(Photo by Kyle Edwards)

Move along, measuring as you go, until you've linked the entire sausage casing.

Look ahead as you link the last two or three sausages, and either make them bigger or smaller to avoid having one very small sausage. After you've linked the last sausage, knot the end of the casing. There should be about $\frac{1}{4}$ to $\frac{1}{2}$ inch between each twisted casing. At these twists, use kitchen sheers or a knife to cut between each link.

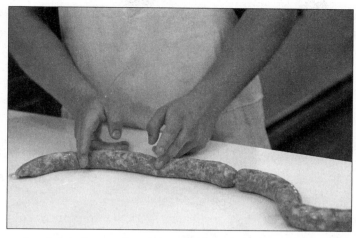

Use your hands to estimate where you should link the last two or three sausages so that they are all about the same size.
(Photo by Kyle Edwards)

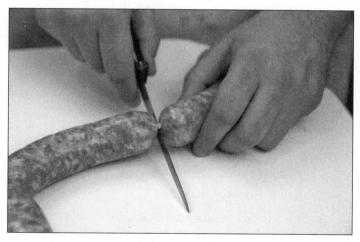

A knife or kitchen sheers make cutting the links an easy task.
(Photo by Kyle Edwards)

Put the individual links in a covered container in the refrigerator or wrap them up to freeze. Wait a day before cooking your links so that all the spices and salts fully blend in with the meat.

After you've packed your links and cleaned your kitchen, you're ready to cook your sausage. For serving and cooking suggestions, check out Chapter 17.

The Least You Need to Know

- After you debone your meat, cube it in $3/4$- to $1^1/_2$-inch cubes.
- Mix spices and salt in with your meat cubes, then chill the sausage mixture in the refrigerator or freezer before grinding.
- Meat grinding plates come in fine, medium, and coarse grades. Grind according to the recipe and your taste.
- If the meat backs up or if gristle gets stuck in the grinder, turn the grinder off, unplug it, clean it, and start again.
- Make a test patty after grinding the meat, but keep in mind that the flavors will intensify within a day of grinding the meat and spices together.
- Slowly crank the meat into the casings, using your thumb on the horn to guide the meat.

Traditional Sausage Recipes

Part

2

This part offers a wide variety of traditional sausage recipes—everything from savory Italian sausage to kielbasas and brats. These are the sausages you may have grown up enjoying and remain some of the most popular commercially produced sausages. But, oh, when you make them yourself, they taste so much better!

Bulk Sausage Recipes

In This Chapter

- Bulk breakfast sausage
- Fancy breakfast sausage
- Italian bulk sausage
- Irish breakfast sausage

Bulk sausages are the easiest type of sausage to make. All you need to do is cut your meat, measure and mix in your spices, and grind the meat and spice mixture. This chapter covers some traditional breakfast sausage recipes, an Italian bulk sausage recipe, and a simple, "mix and go" no-grind recipe.

Bulk sausage is ideal for forming into patties or using in recipes that call for crumbled sausage. You can transform any recipe for link sausages into a recipe for bulk sausages simply by eliminating the linking step from the recipe.

Bulk Breakfast Sausage

This sausage is very simple and tasty. The poultry seasoning and little kick from the black and white pepper will make you feel like you're eating breakfast on a farm.

Yield:	Prep time:	Cook time:	Serving size:
20 (4-ounce) patties	30 minutes	20 minutes	1 patty

2½ TB. kosher salt
2½ tsp. ground white pepper
1½ tsp. ground black pepper
2 tsp. poultry seasoning

5 lb. boneless pork shoulder with up to ½ lb. additional fat if wanted
¾ cup ice water

1. In a small bowl, combine kosher salt, white pepper, black pepper, and poultry seasoning. Set aside.

2. Cut pork into cubes for grinding. Toss with spice mix until evenly dispersed.

3. Store in a covered container in the refrigerator or freezer to chill until you're ready for the next step. Chill mixture for at least 30 minutes to improve grinding quality.

4. Grind mixture through a fine or medium plate (see Chapter 4).

5. Add ice water to ground meat and using your hands or a tabletop mixer, mix until the texture is consistent, about 5 minutes.

6. Make a test patty, cook it, taste it, and adjust seasonings if necessary.

7. Chill mixture in a covered container in the refrigerator or freezer until you're ready for the next step.

8. Form mixture into patties to fry, or package in 1-pound packages for later use. Mixture can also be linked in sheep or hog casing.

Variation: To make a turkey breakfast sausage, try replacing the pork with turkey breasts or using half turkey and half pork.

PRIME CUT

Poultry seasoning usually includes, but isn't limited to, sage, thyme, marjoram, black pepper, celery seed, cayenne pepper, and dehydrated onion. In addition to poultry dishes, poultry seasoning enhances the flavor of pork, veal, meatloaf, herbed breads, and herb sauces.

Fancy Breakfast Sausage

This is similar to the bulk breakfast sausage, but it has a stronger flavor thanks to the fresh herbs, which give it extra zing.

Yield:	Prep time:	Cook time:	Serving size:
12 (5-ounce) links	60 minutes	30 minutes	1 link

2½ TB. kosher salt

1 TB. light brown sugar

2 tsp. ground black pepper

1 tsp. ground white pepper

½ tsp. ground mace

½ tsp. cayenne (optional)

5 lb. boneless pork shoulder with up to ½ lb. additional fat

4 TB. ice water

4 tsp. fresh sage leaves, finely chopped

2 tsp. fresh thyme leaves, finely chopped

1 tsp. fresh rosemary leaves, finely chopped

2 tsp. liquid smoke (optional)

1. In a small bowl, combine kosher salt, light brown sugar, black pepper, white pepper, mace, and cayenne (if using). Set aside.

2. Cut pork into cubes for grinding. Toss with spice mix until evenly dispersed.

3. Store in a covered container in the refrigerator or freezer to chill until you're ready for the next step. Chill mixture for at least 30 minutes to improve grinding quality.

4. Grind mixture through a fine or medium plate (see Chapter 4).

5. Add ice water, sage, thyme, rosemary, and liquid smoke (if using) to ground meat. Using your hands or a tabletop mixer, mix until the texture is consistent, about 5 minutes.

6. Make a test patty, cook it, taste it, and adjust seasonings if necessary.

7. Chill mixture in a covered container in the refrigerator or freezer until you're ready for the next step.

8. Form into patties to fry or package in 1-pound packages for later use. Mixture can also be linked in sheep or hog casing.

Italian Bulk Sausage

Fennel, basil, and garlic flavor this classic sausage. It's perfect for adding to tomato sauces and for topping on pizza.

Yield:	Prep time:	Cook time:	Serving size:
8 (4-ounce) patties	30 minutes	20 minutes	1 patty

1 TB. kosher salt

1 tsp. sugar (optional)

1 tsp. poultry seasoning

1 tsp. ground black pepper

1 tsp. dried basil

1 tsp. garlic powder

1 tsp. fennel seed, cracked or whole (can be added as a garnish)

2 lb. boneless pork shoulder with up to $\frac{1}{2}$ lb. additional fat if wanted

4 TB. ice water

1. In a small bowl, combine kosher salt, sugar (if using), poultry seasoning, black pepper, basil, garlic powder, and fennel seed. Set aside.

2. Cut pork into cubes for grinding. Toss with spice mix until evenly dispersed.

3. Store in a covered container in the refrigerator or freezer to chill until you're ready for the next step. Chill mixture for at least 30 minutes to improve grinding quality.

4. Grind mixture through a fine or medium plate (see Chapter 4).

5. Add ice water to ground meat. Using your hands or a tabletop mixer, mix until the texture is consistent, about 5 minutes.

6. Make a test patty, cook it, taste it, and adjust seasoning if necessary.

7. Chill mixture in a covered container in the refrigerator or freezer until you're ready for the next step.

8. Use mixture in any recipe that calls for Italian sausage or package in 1-pound packages for later use. Mixture can also be linked in sheep or hog casing.

Variation: To make a spicier sausage, add 1 teaspoon cayenne.

CHEF'S CHOICE

Homemade bulk Italian sausage makes a flavorful meatloaf, especially when topped with homemade tomato sauce.

Irish Breakfast Sausage

This Irish twist on the standard bulk breakfast sausage has a more herbaceous flavor and a smoother mouthfeel.

Yield:	Prep time:	Cook time:	Serving size:
12 (5-ounce) links	60 minutes	30 minutes	1 link

2½ TB. kosher salt

2 tsp. ground black pepper

2 tsp. dried thyme leaves

5 lb. boneless pork shoulder with up to ½ lb. additional fat

2 cups panko breadcrumbs

¾ cup milk

2 large eggs

1. In a small bowl, combine kosher salt, black pepper, and thyme. Set aside.

2. Cut pork into cubes for grinding. Toss with spice mix until evenly dispersed.

3. Store in a covered container in the refrigerator or freezer to chill until you're ready for the next step. Chill mixture for at least 30 minutes to improve grinding quality.

4. In a small bowl, soak panko breadcrumbs in milk. Set aside.

5. Grind mixture through a medium plate (see Chapter 4).

6. Add breadcrumb mixture and eggs to ground meat. Using your hands or a table-top mixer, mix until the texture is consistent, about 5 minutes.

7. Make a test patty, cook it, taste it, and adjust seasonings as necessary.

8. Chill mixture in a covered container in the refrigerator or freezer until you're ready for the next step.

9. Form into patties to fry or package in 1-pound packages for later use. Mixture can also be linked in sheep or hog casing.

PRIME CUT

The Irish peasants who created this sausage didn't have a lot of meat, so they added eggs and breadcrumbs as fillers to stretch their meat as far as possible. Today artisan sausage makers add eggs and breadcrumbs to this sausage because they improve the texture of the sausage, giving it a softer mouthfeel.

German Sausages

In This Chapter

- Germany's sausage heritage
- How to make Brühwurst (scalded sausage), Kochwurst (cooked sausage), and Rohwurst (fresh sausage)
- German sausage recipes

Sausages are to Germany's food culture what rice is to China. The country has one of the richest sausage making traditions in the world. More than 1,500 different types of sausage are made in Germany, and sausage is popular at every meal.

This chapter takes you on a tour of Germany's rich history of sausage making and gives you a taste of the different types of meats and styles of German sausages. Once your appetite is whetted for *wurst* (the German word for sausage), you'll get to explore recipes covering some of the most famous and beloved types of German sausage.

Germany's Sausage Heritage

The history of German sausage making goes back at least 1,000 years, and many sausages are made with the same ingredients and methods that have been passed down from generation to generation. Each region in Germany is known for certain types of sausages.

But sausage making as we know it today in Germany has its roots in the Middle Ages. When peasants in Germany began moving toward more urban areas, they began to divide up tasks and specialize in different kinds of work. This, in turn, led to the formation of the four primary guilds in Germany: butchers, bakers, shoemakers, and cloth makers.

Among this group, butchers rose to the top because meat, which was most valued, was also the most challenging to work with. Because of this—and the fact that butchers worked with sharp and pointy objects—butchers were granted permission to carry swords and placed in charge of a city or a town's defenses. These butchers determined who could slaughter meat, who could become butchers, and what prices could be charged for meat. They were basically the who's who of the growing middle class.

> **PRIME CUT**
>
> To see some of the treasure chests, giant knives, and other equipment of medieval butcher guilds, visit the German Butcher Museum in Boblingen, Germany.

Since butchers visited the countryside to purchase pork and beef, they started carrying written correspondence for a fee. As such, they developed Germany's first mail service, called the *metzgerpost*, or "butcher post."

These medieval butchers developed many of Germany's—and the world's—most famous links, including *bratwurst* and frankfurters.

> **DEFINITION**
>
> **Bratwurst** gets its name from *brat*, which means "finely chopped meat," and *wurst*, which means "sausage."

The German butchers' guild survived an 1869 law that weakened the guild system, and the butchers even survived the Industrial Revolution. But today there are fewer butchers than there have ever been.

The rise of supermarkets in the 1980s really decimated the profession. In the 1970s, there were about 70,000 butchers. Today, there are only 17,000, with hundreds retiring every year.

Germans still eat a lot of sausages and meat—about 100 pounds per person per year. But most of it's mass-produced by factories, which churn out identical, machine-produced product, including sausages that are molded into animal shapes for children.

A Brief Primer on German Sausages

Each region of Germany has its own special kinds of sausages, from sardine sausages made in the north along the North and Baltic seas, to the veal and pork sausages of Bavaria.

In Germany, sausages are made from pork, veal, beef, poultry, and seafood. Some sausages also incorporate blood and/or organ meats. Most sausages, however, are made from pork, or a blend of pork and other meats. The second most popular sausage meat is veal.

PRIME CUT

The bratwurst was so important to Germany that in the fifteenth century the government issued a "bratwurst purity law" that basically outlawed the use of bad meat in the sausage.

German sausages are highly spiced, often containing cardamom, nutmeg, pepper, coriander, ginger, and Hungarian paprika. They also use fresh parsley and other herbs.

German sausages generally fall into the following primary categories, based on how they are prepared:

- **Brühwurst:** Scalded sausage
- **Kochwurst:** Cooked sausage
- **Rohwurst:** Fresh sausage

Scalded sausages are boiled or scalded in hot water, and they are a type of fresh sausage. Cooked sausages include liver sausage and blood sausage. Fresh sausages are the most popular kind of sausages in Germany, with more than 600 different varieties, including the many variations of bratwurst.

The recipes that follow in this chapter are all fresh (Rohwurst) or scalded (Brühwurst).

Basic German Bratwurst

This recipe for a standard German bratwurst is one of our all-time favorite sausage recipes. The flavor of the sage shines through the base peppery flavor of this sausage, which is distinct without being overpowering.

Yield:	Prep time:	Cook time:	Serving size:
15 (5-ounce) links	60 minutes	30 minutes	1 link

2½ TB. kosher salt

1½ TB. rubbed sage

2½ tsp. ground white pepper

1½ tsp. ground black pepper

¼ tsp. ground mace

¼ tsp. ground celery seed

5 lb. boneless pork shoulder with up to ½ lb. additional fat

¾ cup ice water

10 ft. hog casing or 32 mm collagen casing

1. In a small bowl, combine kosher salt, sage, white pepper, black pepper, mace, and celery seed. Set aside.

2. Cut pork into cubes for grinding. Toss with spice mix until evenly dispersed.

3. Store in a covered container in the refrigerator or freezer to chill until you're ready for the next step. Chill mixture for at least 30 minutes to improve grinding quality.

4. Grind mixture through a fine or medium plate (see Chapter 4).

5. Add ice water to ground meat. Using your hands or a tabletop mixer, mix until the texture is consistent, about 5 minutes.

6. Make a test patty, cook it, taste it, and adjust seasonings if necessary.

7. Chill mixture in a covered container in the refrigerator or freezer until you're ready for the next step.

8. Stuff mixture in hog or collagen casing (see Chapter 4).

PRIME CUT

Besides the bratwurst we are most familiar with, some versions in Germany are made with beef or veal, and still others have wine added.

Thüringer Sausage

Thüringer sausages are similar to bratwursts, but they have a milder, more subtle flavor. This is a perfectly balanced German classic.

Yield:	Prep time:	Cook time:	Serving size:
12 (5-ounce) links	60 minutes	30 minutes	1 link

2 TB. kosher salt

2 tsp. rubbed marjoram

1 tsp. ground coriander

1 tsp. ground caraway seed

1 tsp. lemon zest (1 lemon) or to taste

½ tsp. ground black pepper

½ tsp. ground white pepper

½ tsp. ground mace

½ tsp. onion powder

½ tsp. garlic powder

4 lb. boneless pork shoulder with up to ½ lb. additional fat

⅓ cup milk, 2 percent or whole

¼ cup. ice water

8 ft. hog casing or 32 mm collagen casing

1. In a small bowl, combine kosher salt, marjoram, coriander, caraway seed, lemon zest, black pepper, white pepper, mace, onion powder, and garlic powder. Set aside.

2. Cut pork into cubes for grinding. Toss with spice mix until evenly dispersed.

3. Store in a covered container in the refrigerator or freezer to chill until you're ready for the next step. Chill mixture for at least 30 minutes to improve grinding quality.

4. Grind mixture through a fine or medium plate (see Chapter 4).

5. Add milk and ice water to ground meat. Using your hands or a tabletop mixer, mix until the texture is consistent, about 5 minutes.

6. Make a test patty, cook it, taste it, and adjust seasonings if necessary.

7. Chill mixture in a covered container in the refrigerator or freezer until you're ready for the next step.

8. Stuff mixture in hog or collagen casing (see Chapter 4).

CHEF'S CHOICE

To make a lighter color and flavor, many sausage makers add veal to their Thüringer. Simply reduce the amount of pork to 3 pounds and add 1 pound veal.

Nürnberg-Style Bratwurst

This is one of many regional variations of bratwurst. Unlike traditional brats, it's heavily spiced, with strong notes of cardamom and ginger.

Yield:	Prep time:	Cook time:	Serving size:
12 (5-ounce) links	60 minutes	30 minutes	1 link

2 TB. kosher salt

4 tsp. ground caraway seed

½ tsp. ground mace

½ tsp. ground white pepper

¼ tsp. ground ginger

¼ tsp. ground allspice

¼ tsp. ground celery seed

⅛ tsp. ground cardamom

4 lb. boneless pork shoulder with up to ½ lb. additional fat

2 tsp. liquid smoke or to taste

⅔ cup ice water

8 ft. hog casing or 32 mm collagen casing

1. In a small bowl, combine kosher salt, caraway seed, mace, white pepper, ginger, allspice, celery seed, and cardamom. Set aside.

2. Cut pork into cubes for grinding. Toss with spice mix until evenly dispersed.

3. Store in a covered container in the refrigerator or freezer to chill until you're ready for the next step. Chill mixture for at least 30 minutes to improve grinding quality.

4. Grind mixture through a fine or medium plate (see Chapter 4).

5. Add liquid smoke and ice water to ground meat. Using your hands or a tabletop mixer, mix until the texture is consistent, about 5 minutes.

6. Make a test patty, cook it, taste it, and adjust seasonings if necessary.

7. Chill mixture in a covered container in the refrigerator or freezer until you're ready for the next step.

8. Stuff mixture in hog or collagen casing (see Chapter 4).

PRIME CUT

This sausage is traditionally served with mashed potatoes, sauerkraut, and a dollop or two of horseradish cream.

Weisswurst

Weisswurst is a Bavarian favorite. Savory, with just a hint of sweetness, this "white sausage" is just delicious.

Yield:	Prep time:	Cook time:	Serving size:
15 (5-ounce) links	60 minutes	30 minutes	1 link

2 TB. kosher salt

1 TB. sugar

¼ cup nonfat dry milk

1 TB. ground mustard seed

1½ tsp. ground white pepper

½ tsp. ground celery seed

½ tsp. ground mace

½ tsp. onion powder

½ tsp. dried parsley

3 lb. boneless veal shoulder (also called "stew meat" when cubed)

2 lb. boneless pork shoulder (don't add fat)

1½ cup ice water

10 ft. hog casing or 32 mm collagen casing

1. In a small bowl, combine kosher salt, sugar, dry milk, mustard seed, white pepper, celery seed, mace, onion powder, and parsley. Set aside.

2. Cut veal and pork into cubes for grinding. Toss with spice mix until evenly dispersed.

3. Store in a covered container in the refrigerator or freezer to chill until you're ready for the next step. Chill mixture for at least 30 minutes to improve grinding quality.

4. Grind mixture through a fine plate (see Chapter 4).

5. Add ice water to ground meat. Using your hands or a tabletop mixer, mix until the texture is consistent, about 5 minutes.

6. Make a test patty, cook it, taste it, and adjust seasonings as necessary.

7. Chill mixture in a covered container in the refrigerator or freezer until you're ready for the next step.

8. Stuff mixture in hog or collagen casing (see Chapter 4).

PRIME CUT

In Bavaria, Weisswurst is traditionally made early in the morning and consumed as a snack between breakfast and lunch.

Knockwurst Sausage

This beefy sausage is strongly spiced, and it's one of the few sausages in Germany that uses garlic in such large quantities.

Yield:	Prep time:	Cook time:	Serving size:
15 (5-ounce) links	60 minutes	30 minutes	1 link

2½ TB. kosher salt

½ cup nonfat dry milk

1 TB. ground black pepper

1 TB. sweet Spanish paprika

2 tsp. ground mace

½ tsp. ground nutmeg

½ tsp. ground coriander

½ tsp. ground allspice

2½ lb. boneless beef chuck

2½ lb. boneless pork shoulder with additional fat if desired

7 large cloves garlic, finely chopped

¾ cup ice water

10 ft. hog casing or 32 mm collagen casing

1. In a small bowl, combine kosher salt, dry milk, black pepper, sweet Spanish paprika, mace, nutmeg, coriander, and allspice. Set aside.

2. Cut beef and pork into cubes for grinding. Toss with spice mix until evenly dispersed.

3. Store in a covered container in the refrigerator or freezer until you're ready for the next step.

4. Grind mixture through a fine plate (see Chapter 4).

5. Add garlic and ice water to ground meat. Using your hands or a tabletop mixer, mix until the texture is consistent, about 5 minutes.

6. Make a test patty, cook it, taste it, and adjust seasoning as necessary.

7. Chill mixture in a covered container in the refrigerator or freezer until you're ready for the next step.

8. Stuff mixture in hog or collagen casing (see Chapter 4).

PRIME CUT

Knockwurst is traditionally served with sauerkraut and potato salad.

Liverwurst

If you like pâté, then you'll love liverwurst. Creamy and smooth, it's perfect for sandwiches and canapés.

Yield:	Prep time:	Cook time:	Serving size:
6 (5-ounce) links	60 minutes	30 minutes	1 link

2 TB. kosher salt

½ TB. ground black pepper

½ TB. ground white pepper

1 tsp. ground allspice

1 tsp. dried marjoram

½ tsp. rubbed sage

2 lb. boneless pork shoulder with up to ⅓ lb. additional fat

2 lb. fresh pork liver

1 large yellow onion, diced

1 cup ice water

8 ft. hog casing or 38–42 mm collagen casing

1. In a small bowl, combine kosher salt, black pepper, white pepper, allspice, marjoram, and sage. Set aside.

2. Cut pork shoulder and pork liver into cubes for grinding. Toss with spice mix and yellow onion until evenly dispersed.

3. Store in a covered container in the refrigerator or freezer to chill until you're ready for the next step. Chill mixture for at least 30 minutes to improve grinding quality.

4. Grind mixture through a fine plate once for coarse liverwurst or twice for an extra-fine consistency (see Chapter 4).

5. Add ice water to ground meat. Using your hands or a tabletop mixer, mix until the texture is consistent, about 5 minutes.

6. Make a test patty, cook it, taste it, and adjust seasoning as necessary.

7. Chill mixture in a covered container in the refrigerator or freezer until you're ready for the next step.

8. Stuff mixture in hog or collagen casing (see Chapter 4). Links should be small enough to fit in a large pot.

9. Add enough water to a large pot to cover links by several inches. Bring water to a light boil. Place sausages in the pot with one or two large plates over them to keep them submerged. Bring water back to a simmer. Cook sausages until they reach an internal temperature of 155°F, about 1 hour. Use a meat thermometer to determine when sausages are cooked through. Remove liverwurst and plunge into a cold water bath to cool.

Variation: Although usually liver sausages are smooth and creamy, you can also make a coarser, country-style sausage by running the meat through the grinder just once.

PRIME CUT

For an interesting—and strong—sandwich, use pumpernickel bread, red onion, mustard, and limburger cheese. This specialty sandwich is served at Baumgartner's Cheese Store and Tavern in Monroe, Wisconsin.

Italian and Mediterranean Sausages

In This Chapter

- Italy's sausage heritage
- France's sausage heritage
- Sausages from the Mediterranean coast
- Sausage recipes from Italy, France, and the Mediterranean coast

After Germany, Italy has perhaps the richest sausage traditions in Europe. Not only does it have one of the longest heritages, dating back to the Roman Empire, but each region of Italy boasts unique sausages that you won't find anywhere else.

France, while more known for its artisan cheeses, has some strong sausage traditions, too, as do other countries along the Mediterranean coast.

This chapter takes you on a culinary tour of Italy's delicious history of sausage making. It also gives you a nibble of France's contributions to sausage and touches upon other Mediterranean sausage making heritages. The chapter closes with a number of scrumptious sausage recipes from these regions.

The Sausage Conquerors

The Romans might not have been the first ancient people to make sausages, but like everything else they did, they made their sausages with panache. From records of their recipes, we know that they made sausages from pork, poultry, squid, mussels, cuttlefish, and even porpoise.

While some of their sausages were common fare, in general, these were highly spiced and exotic endeavors. They exported these sausages—and other culinary inclinations—to the lands they conquered. And besides infiltrating a land's borders, they took over its culinary scene, which they then brought back home and integrated with their own cuisine.

Although the Roman Empire fell in 476, it didn't take the sausages down with it. People of the region, while overrun by various tribes—the Huns, Visigoths, and others during the Middle Ages—continued to make sausage with a vengeance.

As the Romans made all varieties of fresh, cured, and smoked sausages—both linked and unlinked—so did the Italian peoples, before Italy was even a nation. But the people in each region of what is now Italy developed their own sausage making traditions.

The Crusades introduced new spices to Italian sausage makers, and sausage making traditions continued to evolve. Trade routes along the Mediterranean encouraged the development of more salted meat products, especially sausages, which could be transported on long voyages. According to a document from a Spanish ship that was in port at Palermo during 1415, the sailors were fed lamb or pork sausages for at least 13 days out of the month the ship was in port. Interestingly, the sausages were purchased from street vendors.

PRIME CUT

Some famous Italian sausages date back to this time period. Mortadella, for example, may have first appeared on the scene as early as 1376 in Bologna. Bologna is also the birthplace of bologna-style cured meat.

Modern Italian Sausages

Across Italy today, regional sausages abound. Here in the United States, we primarily associate Italy with cured and smoked Italian sausages—such as Mortadella and salami—that are imported here. But that's only because fresh Italian sausages aren't exported.

Sicily and Naples specialize in fresh, sweet pork sausages while Calabrese sausages have a bit of heat.

Though pork remains the meat of choice for many Italian sausages, beef, veal, and wild boar are also used. Tuscany is known for its wild boar sausages that are dried and covered with olive oil.

Italians make plentiful use of garlic, basil, onions, hot peppers, oregano, and other spices to flavor their sausages. Like their Roman ancestors, Italian sausages are highly evolved culinary achievements.

The Saucy Saucissons of France

When the Romans conquered Gaul (what is now France), they took some of the conquered people's sausage making techniques back to Rome. The early French not only dried their sausages, but they smoked them, giving them a signature flavor.

After Rome fell, sausage making evolved in France. By the early seventeenth century, charcuteries, or shops selling cooked meats, were processing pork products of all different kinds. Across France, these charcuteries continue to produce sausages, pâtés, and other meat products of distinguished tastes to this day.

The sausages of France vary from region to region. The Languedoc region in southwest France is influenced by the spicier chorizos of Spain, while the Alsace-Lorraine region boasts several Germanic varieties of sausage, including a *saucisson* (French word for "sausage") de Frankfort, which is not unlike the frankfurters of Frankfort, Germany.

PRIME CUT

Cassoulet is a hearty French casserole that hails from the Langedoc region. It's a stick-to-your-bones meaty affair, an earthen pot filled to the brim with duck, white beans, pork, goose, and sausages.

While the French produce both fresh and cured sausages, most sausages are considered country cooking, rather than haute cuisine.

Sausages in France are highly spiced affairs made with everything from chestnuts and caramelized sugar to wines and mustards. Although pork is popular, so are veal, beef, poultry, seafood, and even goat—the latter sausages can be found in some small villages in Burgundy.

A Sea of Sausages

Across the various lands that border the Mediterranean Sea, including Greece and Morocco, you'll find dozens of sausage varieties. More than 90 different types of sausages hail from this region, including everything from Asturiana, a Spanish blood and bacon sausage, to Zampone, an Italian pork meat stuffed into a pig's trotter sausage (sausage made by stuffing the sausage meat into the foot of a hog).

The roots of sausage making in these countries go back to at least Roman times—again, those culinary conquerors left their footprints entwined in sausage links. But most of the sausages you'll find today in these countries first appeared on the scene during the Middle Ages. Historically, they were first made by farm families and peasants, and then, when people moved to urban areas, specialized sausage makers and peddlers began making and refining them.

Pork meat was popular, but beef, seafood, and lamb were also ground into sausage. Ingredients also included garlic, peppers, oregano, lemon, ginger, and other spices.

Sweet Italian Sausage

Although fennel seed is used in many Italian sausage recipes, the larger quantity in this recipe, along with sugar, teases out the sweetness in the pork.

Yield:	Prep time:	Cook time:	Serving size:
15 (5-ounce) links	60 minutes	30 minutes	1 link

2½ TB. kosher salt

1 TB. sugar

1½ TB. ground black pepper

2 TB. fennel seed, whole or cracked

1 tsp. sweet Spanish paprika

½ tsp. garlic powder

5 lb. boneless pork shoulder with up to ½ lb. additional fat

¾ cup ice water

10 ft. hog casing or 32 mm collagen casing

1. In a small bowl, combine kosher salt, sugar, black pepper, fennel seed, sweet Spanish paprika, and garlic powder. Set aside.

2. Cut pork into cubes for grinding and place in a large mixing bowl or hotel pan.

3. Store in a covered container in the refrigerator or freezer until you're ready for the next step. Chill mixture for at least 30 minutes to improve grinding quality.

4. Grind mixture through a medium plate (see Chapter 4).

5. Add ice water to ground meat. Using your hands or a tabletop mixer, mix until the texture is consistent, about 5 minutes.

6. Make a test patty, cook it, taste it, and adjust seasonings as necessary.

7. Chill mixture in a covered container in the refrigerator or freezer until you're ready for the next step.

8. Stuff mixture in hog or collagen casing (see Chapter 4).

 THE GRIND

Make sure you use the exact type of paprika called for in a recipe. Hungarian paprikas are typically more mild than Spanish paprikas. And hot Spanish paprikas are typically much stronger than their sweet Spanish counterparts.

Hot Italian Sausage

Hot Spanish paprika and cayenne give this sausage a spicy kick.

Yield:	Prep time:	Cook time:	Serving size:
12 (5-ounce) links	60 minutes	30 minutes	1 link

3 TB. kosher salt

1 TB. sugar

3 TB. ground black pepper

½ TB. fennel seed, whole or cracked

2 TB. sweet Spanish paprika

½ tsp. ground cayenne

1 TB. red pepper flakes

5 lb. boneless pork shoulder with up to ½ lb. additional fat

¾ cup ice water

10 ft. hog casing or 32 mm collagen casing

1. In a small bowl, combine kosher salt, sugar, black pepper, fennel seed, sweet Spanish paprika, cayenne, and red pepper flakes. Set aside.

2. Cut pork into cubes for grinding and place in a large mixing bowl or hotel pan.

3. Using your hands or a wooden spoon, toss meat with spice mix until spices are evenly dispersed. Store in a covered container in the refrigerator or freezer until you're ready for the next step. Chill mixture for at least 30 minutes to improve grinding quality.

4. Grind mixture through a medium plate (see Chapter 4).

5. Add ice water to ground meat. Using your hands or a tabletop mixer, mix until the texture is consistent, about 5 minutes.

6. Make a test patty, cook it, taste it, and adjust seasonings as necessary.

7. Chill mixture in a covered container in the refrigerator or freezer until you're ready for the next step.

8. Stuff mixture in hog or collagen casing (see Chapter 4).

CHEF'S CHOICE

You can increase the quantity of red pepper flakes to reach the desired level of heat. For a really spicy hot Italian sausage, increase the amount of red pepper flakes to 2 tablespoons.

Tuscan Country-Style Italian Sausage

This rustic sausage is sweet and aromatic, as it's laced with cinnamon, cloves, and mace.

Yield:	Prep time:	Cook time:	Serving size:
12 (5-ounce) links	60 minutes	30 minutes	1 link

2½ TB. kosher salt

1 TB. sugar

1½ tsp. ground black pepper

3 cloves fresh garlic, finely chopped

½ tsp. ground mace

½ tsp. ground coriander

¼ tsp. ground cayenne

⅛ tsp. ground cloves

⅛ tsp. ground cinnamon

5 lb. boneless pork shoulder with up to ½ lb. additional fat

⅔ cup ice water

10 ft. hog casing or 32 mm collagen casing

1. In a small bowl, combine kosher salt, sugar, black pepper, garlic, mace, coriander, cayenne, cloves, and cinnamon. Set aside.

2. Cut pork into cubes for grinding and place in a large mixing bowl or hotel pan.

3. Using your hands or a wooden spoon, toss meat with spice mix until spices are evenly dispersed. Store in a covered container in the refrigerator or freezer until you're ready for the next step. Chill mixture for at least 30 minutes to improve grinding quality.

4. Grind mixture through a medium plate (see Chapter 4).

5. Add ice water to ground meat. Using your hands or a tabletop mixer, mix until the texture is consistent, about 5 minutes.

6. Make a test patty, cook it, taste it, and adjust seasonings as necessary.

7. Chill mixture in a covered container in the refrigerator or freezer until you're ready for the next step.

8. Stuff mixture in hog or collagen casing (see Chapter 4).

PRIME CUT

This sausage tastes great when added to pizza, calzones, or foccacia bread.

Sicilian Sausage

Red wine and Pecorino Romano cheese give this sausage its distinctive flavor.

Yield:	Prep time:	Cook time:	Serving size:
13 (5-ounce) links	60 minutes	30 minutes	1 link

2 TB. kosher salt

2 tsp. ground black pepper

2 TB. fennel seed, cracked or whole

2 tsp. red pepper flakes

4 lb. boneless pork shoulder with up to ½ lb. additional fat

1 cup finely grated Pecorino Romano or Parmigiano-Reggiano cheese

1 cup dry red wine, preferably Sicilian or Italian

8 ft. hog casing or 32 mm collagen casing

1. In a small bowl, combine kosher salt, black pepper, fennel seed, and red pepper flakes. Set aside.

2. Cut pork into cubes for grinding and place in a large mixing bowl or hotel pan.

3. Using your hands or a wooden spoon, toss meat with spice mix until spices are evenly dispersed. Store in a covered container in the refrigerator or freezer until you're ready for the next step. Chill mixture for at least 30 minutes to improve grinding quality.

4. Grind mixture through a medium plate (see Chapter 4).

5. Add Pecorino Romano cheese and red wine to ground meat. Using your hands or a tabletop mixer, mix until the texture is consistent, about 5 minutes.

6. Make a test patty, cook it, taste it, and adjust seasonings as necessary.

7. Chill mixture in a covered container in the refrigerator or freezer until you're ready for the next step.

8. Stuff mixture in hog or collagen casing (see Chapter 4).

THE GRIND

Any time you cook with wine or beer, make sure you use one you'd actually drink. If you don't like how a wine or beer tastes, you won't like the flavor it adds to your sausage.

French Fresh Garlic Sausage

If you like garlic and onions, you'll love this sausage, which is chock full of them.

Yield:	Prep time:	Cook time:	Serving size:
18 (5-ounce) links	60 minutes	30 minutes	1 link

3 TB. kosher salt

2 tsp. ground black pepper

1 tsp. dried thyme

$\frac{1}{8}$ tsp. ground bay leaf

4 lb. boneless pork shoulder with up to $\frac{1}{2}$ lb. additional fat

2 lb. boneless beef chuck

1 small yellow onion, diced

$\frac{1}{2}$ cup fresh garlic

$\frac{3}{4}$ cup ice water

12 ft. hog casing or 32 mm collagen casing

1. In a small bowl, combine kosher salt, black pepper, thyme, and bay leaf. Set aside.

2. Cut pork and beef into cubes for grinding and place in a large mixing bowl or hotel pan.

3. Using your hands or a wooden spoon, toss meat with spice mix, yellow onion, and garlic until they are evenly dispersed. Store in a covered container in the refrigerator or freezer until you're ready for the next step. Chill mixture for at least 30 minutes to improve grinding quality.

4. Grind mixture through a fine or medium plate (see Chapter 4).

5. Add ice water to ground meat. Using your hands or a tabletop mixer, mix until the texture is consistent, about 5 minutes.

6. Make a test patty, cook it, taste it, and adjust seasonings as necessary.

7. Chill mixture in a covered container in the refrigerator or freezer until you're ready for the next step.

8. Stuff mixture in hog or collagen casing (see Chapter 4).

CHEF'S CHOICE

You can make an all-pork sausage by using 6 pounds pork, or you can increase the ratio of beef to pork by using 4 pounds beef and 2 pounds pork.

Greek Loukaniko Sausage

This sausage zips with fresh parsley, orange zest, and garlic. It's highly aromatic and quite delicious.

Yield:	Prep time:	Cook time:	Serving size:
15 (5-ounce) links	60 minutes	30 minutes	1 link

1 medium onion, chopped

1 tsp. garlic, finely chopped

2½ TB. kosher salt

2 TB. orange zest

2 tsp. ground black pepper

½ tsp. ground bay leaf

½ tsp. ground allspice

½ tsp. crushed red pepper flakes

½ tsp. cayenne

2 tsp. dried oregano

½ tsp. dried thyme

5 lb. boneless pork shoulder with up to ½ lb. additional fat

⅔ cup ice water

1 TB. fresh flat-leaf parsley, finely chopped

10 ft. hog casing or 32 mm collagen casing

1. In a small frying pan over medium heat, sauté onion and garlic in 2 teaspoons olive oil until lightly browned, about 7 minutes. Remove to a medium bowl to cool.

2. In a small bowl, combine kosher salt, orange zest, black pepper, bay leaf, allspice, red pepper flakes, cayenne, oregano, and thyme. Set aside.

3. Cut pork into cubes for grinding and place in a large mixing bowl or hotel pan.

4. Using your hands or a wooden spoon, toss meat with spice mix and sautéed onion and garlic until they are evenly dispersed. Store in a covered container in the refrigerator or freezer until you're ready for the next step. Chill mixture for at least 30 minutes to improve grinding quality.

5. Grind mixture through a fine or medium plate (see Chapter 4).

6. Add ice water and parsley to ground meat. Using your hands or a tabletop mixer, mix until the texture is consistent, about 5 minutes.

7. Make a test patty, cook it, taste it, and adjust seasonings as necessary.

8. Chill mixture in a covered container in the refrigerator or freezer until you're ready for the next step. Chill mixture for at least 30 minutes to improve grinding quality.

9. Stuff mixture in hog or collagen casing (see Chapter 4).

African Boerewors Sausage

This delicious sausage tastes strongly of coriander and brandy, and it's accented by sweet cloves and mace.

Yield:	Prep time:	Cook time:	Serving size:
18 (5-ounce) links	60 minutes	30 minutes	1 link

3 TB. kosher salt

3 TB. ground coriander

2 tsp. ground black pepper

$\frac{1}{4}$ tsp. ground cloves

$\frac{1}{2}$ tsp. ground mace

4 lb. boneless beef chuck

2 lb. boneless pork shoulder with up to $\frac{1}{3}$ lb. additional fat

$\frac{1}{2}$ cup red wine vinegar

2 TB. brandy

$\frac{1}{4}$ cup ice water

12 ft. hog casing or 32 mm collagen casing

1. In a small bowl, combine kosher salt, coriander, black pepper, cloves, and mace. Set aside.

2. Cut beef and pork into cubes for grinding and place in a large mixing bowl or hotel pan.

3. Using your hands or a wooden spoon, toss meat with spice mix until spices are evenly dispersed. Store in a covered container in the refrigerator or freezer until you're ready for the next step. Chill mixture for at least 30 minutes to improve grinding quality.

4. Grind mixture through a medium plate (see Chapter 4).

5. Add red wine vinegar, brandy, and ice water to ground meat. Using your hands or a tabletop mixer, mix until the texture is consistent, about 5 minutes.

6. Make a test patty, cook it, taste it, and adjust seasonings as necessary.

7. Chill mixture in a covered container in the refrigerator or freezer until you're ready for the next step.

8. Stuff mixture in hog or collagen casing (see Chapter 4).

PRIME CUT

Though this sausage originated in Africa, it has its roots in the Netherlands. It's also a popular sausage in Great Britain and Australia. There's a garlic version of boerewors as well as a similar sausage made with kudu, a type of antelope.

Moroccan Sausage

This exotic lamb and beef sausage is sweetened with currants and pomegranate juice, which are perfectly accented by fresh garlic and cilantro.

Yield:	Prep time:	Cook time:	Serving size:
18 (5-ounce) links	60 minutes	30 minutes	1 link

3 TB. kosher salt

1 TB. ground black pepper

1 tsp. ground cumin

1 tsp. ground coriander

1 tsp. ground allspice

1 tsp. dried thyme

½ tsp. ground cinnamon

4 lb. boneless lamb shoulder, trimmed of excess fat

2 lb. boneless beef chuck

1 TB. garlic, finely chopped

3 TB. fresh cilantro, chopped

1 cup currants

1 cup pomegranate juice, chilled

12 ft. hog casing or 32 mm collagen casing

1. In a small bowl, combine kosher salt, black pepper, cumin, coriander, allspice, thyme, and cinnamon. Set aside.

2. Cut lamb and beef into cubes for grinding and place in a large mixing bowl or hotel pan.

3. Using your hands or a wooden spoon, toss meat with spice mix and garlic until they are evenly dispersed. Store in a covered container in the refrigerator or freezer until you're ready for the next step. Chill mixture for at least 30 minutes to improve grinding quality.

4. Grind mixture through a fine or medium plate (see Chapter 4).

5. Add cilantro, currants, and pomegranate juice to ground meat. Using your hands or a tabletop mixer, mix until the texture is consistent, about 5 minutes.

6. Make a test patty, cook it, taste it, and adjust seasonings as necessary.

7. Chill mixture in a covered container in the refrigerator or freezer until you're ready for the next step.

8. Stuff mixture in hog or collagen casing (see Chapter 4).

Polish and Eastern European Sausages

In This Chapter

- Poland's sausage heritage
- Lithuania's sausage heritage
- The rest of Eastern Europe's sausage heritage
- Sausage recipes from Poland and Eastern Europe

Poland and Eastern Europe have a rich sausage making heritage, and their sausages are well-known throughout the world.

Kielbasas, anyone?

After sampling some highlights of sausage making history in Poland and Eastern Europe, this chapter provides recipes so you can make your own artisan Polish and Eastern European sausages.

Polish Sausage Heritage

The history of Polish sausage making goes back about a thousand years. Archaeological evidence suggests that trade merchants from Rome and other regions visited what's now Poland perhaps as early as 500 B.C.E., following what was known as the Amber Route to get amber by the Baltic Sea. However, we don't know exactly what they traded.

It's safe to assume that if the Romans were around, sausages were also being made. Though these earliest traders didn't leave many records behind, ties between Rome and Poland strengthened in 966 C.E., when Poland became a Christian nation, and

Rome's emperor of that era actually came to visit Poland's king. The two rulers wined and dined each other, and sausages were involved in the culinary and cultural exchange.

During the Middle Ages, the two big sausage makers were monks and tradesmen, and this is really when the first Polish sausages that we'd recognize appeared on the scene.

In 1646, Polish King Mieczyslaw IW married a French princess, Ludwika Maria Gonzaga, and not only did she add a dash of sophistication to Polish cuisine overall, but she introduced Poland to pâtés. Liver sausages became more popular as a result.

Around this time, the first evidence of *kielbasa* emerges. The kielbasa of the eighteenth century was a thick sausage, heavily smoked and a few feet in length. Merchants began carrying it with them, and knights riding horses could be seen carrying them roped around their belts.

DEFINITION

Kielbasa means "sausage" in Polish, and the sausage we refer to in the United States as a kielbasa actually is called a krakowska, or Krakow-style sausage, in Poland.

Though the sausages of this time were primarily made of pork, Poles also added wild boar, deer, and rabbit meat to their sausages.

Communists, Solidarity, and Sausage Making

Modern Polish sausage making really began with rebuilding after World War II. One of the goals of the new Communist government was to rebuild Poland's once great meat-packing industry. Besides rebuilding its herds and factories, it categorized all of Poland's sausages. Until 1945, a sausage of the same name in Poland was made in dozens or more variations. The Communist government standardized these variations based on time-honored recipes.

The first official guide to meat products was published in 1959, categorizing 46 sausages and 13 liver and blood sausages. In 1964, the update contained 119 sausages, 19 liver and blood sausages, and 11 pâtés and meat loaves.

PRIME CUT

Under the new Communist guidelines, the only chemical allowed in any of the Polish meats, including sausages and hams, was potassium nitrate.

This standardization allowed Polish sausage makers to produce sausages of high and consistent quality. In a sense, the Communist "Department of Meat Industry" trade-marked Polish sausages, hams, and other meat products. If a sausage was to be called Kabanosy (a cured and dried meat stick particular to the eastern region of Poland), it had to meet certain requirements.

When Lech Walesa and Solidarity rose in Poland, Communists and their meat-packing department were shown the door. Democracy and capitalism was a boon to the country, but not to its meat products and sausages. The sausage aficionados say that new factories started adding chemicals and additives, and their country's once high-quality sausages went downhill from there. However, within the last 10 years there's been a resurgent interest in artisan products in Poland, and the country even hosts an annual artisanal sausage making conference.

Lithuanian Sausage Heritage

What is today called Lithuania was part of Poland at one time. Lithuania was known for smoked meats, and it also had some very distinct methods of rearing pigs and then processing the hog meat.

Lithuanian hogs were mainly fed rye, barley, and potatoes; in some cases, they were fed only flour. Such fare made the hog meat more tender and gave it a sweeter flavor. The hogs were also butchered with a simple stab to the heart, and the wound was then plugged with a piece of wood so that the blood wouldn't run out, which imparted a dark red color to the meat. The hair wasn't removed from the skin by boiling. Instead, hay was burned around the outside of the hog carcass, and then the hair was scraped off.

They also stuffed some sausages with juniper berries; the jalawcowa sausage, the most well-known Lithuanian sausage, has a distinctive flavor because of these spicy berries.

Other Eastern European Sausage Heritages

Hungary, the Czech and Slovak republics, the Ukraine, and the former states of the U.S.S.R. all have their own unique sausage heritages. But as a group, their sausages are more similar to those of Poland than to Germany.

Like both Germany and Poland, most of the sausages are created from pork, but some beef, game animals, and even poultry are used. Hungarians, in particular, grind a wide variety of meats into sausage.

People in these states eat sausages, often served with mustard or horseradish sauce, for every meal.

Flavors of Polish and Eastern European Sausages

The predominant flavors in most Polish and Eastern European sausages are onion and garlic. In fact, the main difference between these sausages and German sausages is the heavy influence of garlic.

Eastern Europeans also use small quantities of allspice, black pepper, and other spices, but the main flavors you'll taste when you bite into these sausages are garlic and onions. The exception, however, is the sausages made with paprika, which typically overpowers the other spices.

Fresh Polish Kielbasa

This kielbasa is a fresh sausage with a mild, garlicky flavor that comes out in every bite.

Yield:	Prep time:	Cook time:	Serving size:
15 (5-ounce) links	60 minutes	30 minutes	1 link

2 TB. kosher salt

1 TB. yellow mustard seed, crushed

1¼ tsp. ground black pepper

1 tsp. garlic powder

¾ tsp. ground allspice

¾ tsp. ground celery seed

5 lb. boneless pork shoulder with up to ½ lb. additional fat

¾ cup ice water

10 ft. hog casing or 32 mm collagen casing

1. In a small bowl, combine kosher salt, yellow mustard seed, black pepper, garlic powder, allspice, and celery seed. Set aside.

2. Cut pork into cubes for grinding and place in a large mixing bowl or hotel pan.

3. Using your hands or a wooden spoon, toss meat with spice mix until spices are evenly dispersed. Store in a covered container in the refrigerator or freezer until you're ready for the next step. Chill mixture for at least 30 minutes to improve grinding quality.

4. Grind mixture through a fine or medium plate (see Chapter 4).

5. Add ice water to ground meat. Using your hands or a tabletop mixer, mix until the texture is consistent, about 5 minutes.

6. Make a test patty, cook it, taste it, and adjust seasonings as necessary.

7. Chill mixture in a covered container in the refrigerator or freezer until you're ready for the next step.

8. Stuff mixture in hog or collagen casing (see Chapter 4).

CHEF'S CHOICE

Kielbasa is traditionally served with sauerkraut, but it also makes a great addition to potato soup, au gratin potatoes, and other potato dishes.

Hungarian Kolbasz Sausage

This sweet sausage packs a wallop of paprika.

Yield:	Prep time:	Cook time:	Serving size:
12 (5-ounce) links	60 minutes	30 minutes	1 link

2 TB. kosher salt

2 TB. sweet Hungarian paprika

1½ tsp. ground allspice

½ tsp. garlic powder

¼ tsp. red pepper flakes

4 lb. boneless pork shoulder with up to ½ lb. additional fat

⅔ cup ice water

8 ft. hog casing or 32 mm collagen casing (optional)

1. In a small bowl, combine kosher salt, sweet Hungarian paprika, allspice, garlic powder, and red pepper flakes. Set aside.

2. Cut pork into cubes for grinding and place in a large mixing bowl or hotel pan.

3. Using your hands or a wooden spoon, toss meat with spice mix until spices are evenly dispersed. Store in a covered container in the refrigerator or freezer until you're ready for the next step. Chill mixture for at least 30 minutes to improve grinding quality.

4. Grind mixture through a fine or medium plate (see Chapter 4).

5. Add ice water to ground meat. Using your hands or a tabletop mixer, mix until the texture is consistent, about 5 minutes.

6. Make a test patty, cook it, taste it, and adjust seasonings as necessary.

7. Chill mixture in a covered container in the refrigerator or freezer until you're ready for the next step.

8. Stuff mixture in hog or collagen casing (if using; see Chapter 4) or use as bulk sausage.

CHEF'S CHOICE

Hungarian Kolbasz tastes great grilled, but it also adds nice flavor to casseroles and stews. No matter how you cook it, be sure to use sweet Hungarian paprika in this recipe rather than Spanish paprika, because Hungarian is sweeter and milder in flavor.

Fresh Lithuanian Kielbasa

This kielbasa is dominated by the sweet yet savory flavor of onion.

Yield:	Prep time:	Cook time:	Serving size:
12 (5-ounce) links	60 minutes	30 minutes	1 link

2 TB. kosher salt

1 tsp. ground allspice

1/4 tsp. ground black pepper

1/2 lb. yellow onion, chopped

4 lb. boneless pork shoulder with up to 1/2 lb. additional fat

2/3 cup ice water

10 ft. hog casing or 32 mm collagen casing (optional)

1. In a small bowl, combine kosher salt, allspice, and black pepper. Set aside.

2. Cut pork into cubes for grinding and place in a large mixing bowl or hotel pan.

3. Using your hands or a wooden spoon, toss meat with spice mix until spices are evenly dispersed. Store in a covered container in the refrigerator or freezer until you're ready for the next step. Chill mixture for at least 30 minutes to improve grinding quality.

4. Grind mixture through a fine or medium plate (see Chapter 4).

5. Add yellow onion and ice water to ground meat. Using your hands or a tabletop mixer, mix until the texture is consistent, about 5 minutes.

6. Make a test patty, cook it, taste it, and adjust seasonings as necessary.

7. Chill mixture in a covered container in the refrigerator or freezer until you're ready for the next step.

8. Stuff mixture in hog or collagen casing (if using; see Chapter 4) or use as bulk sausage.

CHEF'S CHOICE

This sausage tastes great as a bulk sausage. Make it into large patties and fry it as you would a hamburger. Serve with a dollop of fresh mayo and you'll be in hog heaven.

Serbian Cevapcici Sausage

Similar to some Middle Eastern sausages (keftas), this sausage is unusual in that you don't link it. Instead, you roll it into logs. With an infusion of hot Hungarian paprika, it's the Eastern European equivalent of hot Italian sausage.

Yield:	Prep time:	Cook time:	Serving size:
24 (4-ounce) logs	40 minutes	15 minutes	1 log

$2\frac{1}{2}$ TB. kosher salt

2 TB. hot Hungarian paprika

3 TB. ground black pepper

$\frac{1}{8}$ tsp. ground mace

2 lb. boneless pork shoulder with up to $\frac{1}{2}$ lb. additional fat

2 lb. boneless beef chuck

2 lb. boneless lamb shoulder, trimmed of excess fat

1 cup yellow onion, chopped

1 TB. garlic, finely chopped

Olive oil for cooking

1. In a small bowl, combine kosher salt, hot Hungarian paprika, black pepper, and mace. Set aside.

2. Cut pork, beef, and lamb into cubes for grinding and place in a large mixing bowl or hotel pan.

3. Using your hands or a wooden spoon, toss meat with spice mix until spices are evenly dispersed. Store in a covered container in the refrigerator or freezer until you're ready for the next step. Chill mixture for at least 30 minutes to improve grinding quality.

4. Grind mixture through a fine or medium plate (see Chapter 4).

5. Add yellow onion and garlic to ground meat. Using your hands or a tabletop mixer, mix until combined, about 5 minutes.

6. Make a test patty, cook it, taste it, and adjust seasoning as necessary.

7. Chill mixture in a covered container in the refrigerator or freezer until you're ready for the next step.

8. Roll sausage into rods no bigger than 1 inch in diameter and about 4 inches long. Or for a more consistent shape, use a sausage stuffer with no casings.

9. Brush lightly with olive oil and broil, grill, or pan fry over medium heat for 4 to 5 minutes per side.

CHEF'S CHOICE

Serve these sausages with rice pilaf and vegetables or just wrap in pita bread and top with fresh onions and cucumbers and a dollop of mayo or yogurt.

Czech Beer Sausage

This sausage is similar to kielbasa but the beer gives it a more complex flavor.

Yield:	Prep time:	Cook time:	Serving size:
12 (5-ounce) links	60 minutes	30 minutes	1 link

2 TB. kosher salt

½ tsp. ground black pepper

2 tsp. garlic, finely chopped

1 small yellow onion, diced

4 lb. boneless pork shoulder with up to ½ lb. additional fat

¾ cup. Czech pilsner or other Eastern European beer

8 ft. hog casing or 32 mm collagen casing

1. In a small bowl, combine kosher salt, black pepper, garlic, and yellow onion. Set aside.

2. Cut pork into cubes for grinding and place in a large mixing bowl or hotel pan.

3. Using your hands or a wooden spoon, toss meat with spice mix until spices are evenly dispersed. Store in a covered container in the refrigerator or freezer until you're ready for the next step. Chill mixture for at least 30 minutes to improve grinding quality.

4. Grind mixture through a fine or medium plate (see Chapter 4).

5. Add beer to ground meat. Using your hands or a tabletop mixer, mix until the texture is consistent, about 5 minutes.

6. Make a test patty, cook it, taste it, and adjust seasoning as necessary.

7. Chill mixture in a covered container in the refrigerator or freezer until you're ready for the next step.

8. Stuff mixture in hog or collagen casing (see Chapter 4).

CHEF'S CHOICE

To maximize the beer flavor, simmer these sausages in the same kind of beer you use in the ingredients and then pair them at meal time with the same beer.

Spanish Chorizo and Latin Sausages

In This Chapter

- Spain's chorizo heritage
- Latin America's sausage heritage
- Spanish and Latin sausage recipes

There's nothing quite like chorizo (pronounced *chor-EE-zo*). Spicy and rich, smoky and earthy, this style of sausage is unlike the sausages of Central and Eastern Europe, and it's also different from other sausages made in countries along the Mediterranean Sea. Though chorizo originated in Spain, its culinary cousins are the linguisa (pronounced *lin-gwee-SA*) and chouriço (pronounced *shu-REET-zo*) of Portugul and the chorizos that evolved in the New World.

Chorizos and linguisas are some of the most pungent and tasty sausages on the planet. Some, such as Mexican chorizos, are bursting with an intensity of heat; others, such as linguisa, boast complex flavors with just a little endnote of spice. Still others, like Colombian chorizo, don't have any heat, but instead have a depth of flavor from cumin and other spices. These sausages make great additions to Spanish tapas, Mexican enchiladas, and Portuguese stews; and most of them make incredible bases for nachos, tacos, and chilis.

The Sausage Heritage of the Iberian Peninsula

Segregated from the rest of Europe by mountains and water, Spain and Portugal developed distinct cuisines. But though they were separated, they were often conquered, and the different conquerors—including the Romans, the Moors, and the Greeks—all left their imprint on the cuisine of the region. Thus, you could say, the Spanish chorizo has more of a complicated history than the German bratwurst.

The Romans left behind groves of olives, vineyards, and, of course, sausages and sausage making. While the Romans may not have originated sausage making on the Iberian Peninsula, their more sophisticated techniques most likely advanced sausage making in the region. They, along with the Greeks, also left behind garlic, an integral ingredient in chorizo.

The Moors also left their imprint on Spanish chorizo in the spices they left behind: cinnamon, nutmeg, saffron, and cumin. But more importantly than the culinary traditions was the Spanish reaction to their expulsion in 1492. As almost a reaction to the Moors, who as Muslims didn't eat pork, the Spaniards ate a lot of pork after the Moors departed.

PRIME CUT

To this day, Spaniards eat a lot of pork. In fact, they boast of having the most pork consumption in all of Europe.

The Addition of Paprika

The Spanish and Portuguese aren't the only people who season their pork with garlic, so that's not what sets the sausages of this region apart from their European counterparts. What makes Spanish chorizo and Portuguese linguisa so different is the presence of paprika—Spanish paprika, that is.

Monks in the Caceres region of Southwest Spain developed a technique of smoking and grinding red bell peppers into paprika, or *pimenton* as it's called in Spanish.

Intense and earthy, this spice gives Spanish chorizo—in dozens of its lovely variations—a bright, red-orange glow. It's so predominant an ingredient that sausages without paprika are considered "white chorizos."

Spanish paprika is very different from Hungarian paprika. Whereas Hungarian paprika is the mild paprika your grandmother may sprinkle on her deviled eggs, Spanish paprika has a lot of oomph. Even in its mild or sweet form, it's smoky and has a bit of heat. On the Scoville scale, which measures the heat of different peppers, paprika is on the mild end, but it still can be hot.

Paprika, garlic, and cumin all add a real depth of flavor and nuanced heat to Spanish and Portuguese sausages. These sausages are bursting with rich, savory flavors. And because of the paprika, they add a splash of color to the plate. When you bite into a chorizo or a linguisa, its flavors practically pop into your mouth. Because of their intensity, just a little bit of these sausages can add a lot of flavor into tapas, casseroles, and other dishes.

The Evolution of New World Chorizos

Both the Spanish and the Portuguese explored and conquered parts of North and South America. And they brought their pigs and sausage making techniques with them.

Unlike the chorizos and the linguisas of the Iberian peninsula, the chorizos of the New World weren't always flavored with paprika since it wasn't as readily available in the smoked, dried form. Instead, various chiles and peppers were used to spice the sausages, and many of the sausages evolved to be quite spicy.

Latin American sausage makers added cumin, cilantro, and other fresh herbs to their chorizos, often incorporating the herbs as garnish and studding the links with brilliant green color. The resulting links are fresh-tasting, spicy endeavors!

Fresh Spanish Chorizo

This bright red sausage is smoky and garlicky, with a hint of underlying sweetness.

Yield:	Prep time:	Cook time:	Serving size:
15 (5-ounce) links	60 minutes	30 minutes	1 link

$2\frac{1}{2}$ TB. kosher salt

4 TB. smoked Spanish paprika

1 TB. garlic, finely chopped

2 tsp. ground black pepper

1 tsp. sugar

5 lb. boneless pork shoulder with up to $\frac{1}{2}$ lb. additional fat

$\frac{1}{3}$ cup Spanish red wine or sherry

1 TB. sherry vinegar

10 ft. hog casing or 32 mm collagen casing

1. In a small bowl, combine kosher salt, smoked Spanish paprika, garlic, black pepper, and sugar. Set aside.

2. Cut pork into cubes for grinding and place in a large mixing bowl or hotel pan.

3. Using your hands or a wooden spoon, toss meat with spice mix until spices are evenly dispersed. Store in a covered container in the refrigerator or freezer until you're ready for the next step. Chill mixture for at least 30 minutes to improve grinding quality.

4. Grind mixture through a medium plate (see Chapter 4).

5. Add Spanish red wine and sherry vinegar to ground meat. Using your hands or a tabletop mixer, mix until the texture is consistent, about 5 minutes.

6. Make a test patty, cook it, taste it, and adjust seasoning as necessary.

7. Chill mixture in a covered container in the refrigerator or freezer until you're ready for the next step.

8. Stuff mixture in hog or collagen casing (see Chapter 4).

Variation: Spanish chorizo and Mexican chorizo have very different flavor profiles. If a recipe calls for Spanish chorizo and you don't have it, you're better off substituting Portuguese linguisa. If you need Mexican chorizo in a recipe and don't have it, use a different Latin American chorizo.

Mexican Chorizo

This bright red sausage sings with cumin, cloves, cinnamon, and Mexican oregano.

Yield:	Prep time:	Cook time:	Serving size:
2 pounds bulk or 6 (5-ounce) links	60 minutes	30 minutes	5 ounces bulk or 1 link

2 tsp. kosher salt

2 TB. sweet Spanish paprika

2 TB. chili powder

2 TB ground annatto seed

6 garlic cloves, crushed

1 tsp. Mexican oregano, crushed

1 tsp. ground cumin

1 tsp. ground black pepper

½ tsp. ground cloves

½ tsp. ground cayenne

¼ tsp. ground cinnamon

¼ tsp. ground coriander

¼ tsp. ginger, grated

2 lb. boneless pork shoulder with up to ¼ lb. additional fat

½ cup white vinegar

4 ft. hog casing or 32 mm collagen casing (optional)

1. In a small bowl, combine kosher salt, sweet Spanish paprika, chili powder, annatto seed, garlic, Mexican oregano, cumin, black pepper, cloves, cayenne, cinnamon, coriander, and ginger. Set aside.

2. Cut pork into cubes for grinding and place in a large mixing bowl or hotel pan.

3. Using your hands or a wooden spoon, toss meat with spice mix until spices are evenly dispersed. Store in a covered container in the refrigerator or freezer until you're ready for the next step. Chill mixture for at least 30 minutes to improve grinding quality.

4. Grind mixture through a medium plate (see Chapter 4).

5. Add white vinegar to ground meat. Using your hands or a tabletop mixer, mix until the texture is consistent, about 5 minutes.

6. Make a test patty, cook it, taste it, and adjust seasonings as necessary.

7. Chill mixture in a covered container in the refrigerator or freezer until you're ready for the next step.

8. Stuff in hog or collagen casing (if using; see Chapter 4) or use as bulk sausage.

Argentinean Chorizo

Bacon adds a richness to this chorizo while cloves and nutmeg give it sweetness.

Yield:	Prep time:	Cook time:	Serving size:
2 pounds bulk or 6 (5-ounce) links	60 minutes	30 minutes	5 ounces bulk or 1 link

½ tsp. kosher salt

1 clove garlic, finely chopped

1½ tsp. dried oregano

½ tsp. ground cumin

1½ tsp. ground black pepper

2 tsp. chili powder

¼ tsp. ground cloves

⅛ tsp. ground nutmeg

1½ lb. boneless pork shoulder with no additional fat

½ lb. fresh (unsmoked) bacon, or substitute regular bacon

¾ cup dry white wine

4 ft. hog casing or 32 mm collagen casing (optional)

1. In a small bowl, combine kosher salt, garlic, oregano, cumin, black pepper, chili powder, cloves, and nutmeg. Set aside.

2. Cut pork shoulder and bacon into cubes for grinding and place in a large mixing bowl or hotel pan.

3. Using your hands or a wooden spoon, toss meat with spice mix until spices are evenly dispersed. Store in a covered container in the refrigerator or freezer until you're ready for the next step. Chill mixture for at least 30 minutes to improve grinding quality.

4. Grind mixture through a medium plate (see Chapter 4).

5. Add dry white wine to ground meat. Using your hands or a tabletop mixer, mix until the texture is consistent, about 5 minutes.

6. Make a test patty, cook it, taste it, and adjust seasonings as necessary.

7. Chill mixture in a covered container in the refrigerator or freezer until you're ready for the next step.

8. Stuff in hog or collagen casing (see Chapter 4) or use as bulk sausage.

CHEF'S CHOICE

Use a nice white wine. It doesn't have to be the most expensive bottle on the shelf. To be even more authentic, try the Argentinian wine, Torrontés.

Colombian Chorizo

This is a mild chorizo that's oh-so-savory with an intense cumin flavor.

Yield:	Prep time:	Cook time:	Serving size:
15 (5-ounce) links	60 minutes	30 minutes	1 link

2 TB. kosher salt

1 TB. sugar

1 TB. ground white pepper

4 tsp. ground cumin

1 TB. Spanish sweet paprika

4 lb. boneless pork shoulder with up to ½ lb. additional fat

1 small bunch (3 oz.) green onion, chopped

⅔ cup ice water

8 ft. hog casing or 32 mm collagen casing (optional)

1. In a small bowl, combine kosher salt, sugar, white pepper, cumin, and Spanish sweet paprika. Set aside.

2. Cut pork into cubes for grinding and place in a large mixing bowl or hotel pan.

3. Using your hands or a wooden spoon, toss meat with spice mix until spices are evenly dispersed. Store in a covered container in the refrigerator or freezer until you're ready for the next step. Chill mixture for at least 30 minutes to improve grinding quality.

4. Grind mixture through a medium plate (see Chapter 4).

5. Add green onion and ice water to ground meat. Using your hands or a tabletop mixer, mix until the texture is consistent, about 5 minutes.

6. Make a test patty, cook it, taste it, and adjust seasoning as necessary.

7. Chill mixture in a covered container in the refrigerator or freezer until you're ready for the next step.

8. Stuff mixture in hog or collagen casing (if using; see Chapter 4) or use as bulk sausage.

CHEF'S CHOICE

Colombian chorizo is a great sausage to substitute in recipes that call for Mexican chorizo, especially if you're looking to turn down the heat. It tastes great in tacos, nachos, and other such dishes.

Fresh Portuguese Linguisa

This savory, rich link has a lot going on. Garlic, paprika, and wine mingle with just a touch of cayenne to give it a spicy aftertaste.

Yield:	Prep time:	Cook time:	Serving size:
15 (5-ounce) links	60 minutes	30 minutes	1 link

2½ TB. kosher salt

3 TB. smoked Spanish paprika

2½ TB. garlic, finely chopped

3 tsp. dried oregano

2 tsp. ground white pepper

1 tsp. ground black pepper

1 tsp. sugar

1 tsp. cayenne

5 lb. boneless pork shoulder with up to ½ lb. additional fat

¾ cup Spanish red wine, such as Rioja

10 ft. hog casing or 32 mm collagen casing

1. In a small bowl, combine kosher salt, smoked Spanish paprika, garlic, oregano, white pepper, black pepper, sugar, and cayenne. Set aside.

2. Cut pork into cubes for grinding and place in a large mixing bowl or hotel pan.

3. Using your hands or a wooden spoon, toss meat with spice mix until spices are evenly dispersed. Store in a covered container in the refrigerator or freezer until you're ready for the next step. Chill mixture for at least 30 minutes to improve grinding quality.

4. Grind mixture through a medium plate (see Chapter 4).

5. Add Spanish red wine to ground meat. Using your hands or a tabletop mixer, mix until the texture is consistent, about 5 minutes.

6. Make a test patty, cook it, taste it, and adjust seasoning as necessary.

7. Chill mixture in a covered container in the refrigerator or freezer until you're ready for the next step.

8. Stuff mixture in hog or collagen casing (see Chapter 4).

CHEF'S CHOICE

This sausage is great to stuff in empanadas, blend with honey for a spread, or just stuff in a bun. Be sure to use a fine red wine—Spanish or Portuguese. It is also a great sausage to substitute in recipes that call for Spanish chorizo, since it is a close cousin.

English and American Sausages

In This Chapter

- Britain's sausage heritage
- America's sausage heritage
- British and American sausage recipes

People living in the British Isles and the United States have long loved sausages, and both have a long and delicious history of consuming them. A traditional English breakfast wouldn't be complete without sausages—even the recent British royal wedding between Prince William and Catherine Middleton featured sausages as part of the meal. In the United States, no barbecue or baseball game is complete without sausage, whether in the form of a hot dog slathered in mustard, onions, and relish or a juicy sausage washed down with a cold beer.

British sausages tend to be straightforward, and you can really taste the quality of the meat in these sausages because they're more mildly spiced. Spices like nutmeg, mace, and sage accentuate the meat without overwhelming it. And because the Brits like to add breadcrumbs to their sausages, they are quite tender to the tooth.

In addition to the humble hotdog, the andouille sausage is a distinctly American affair. What was once a more refined and mild sausage in France has evolved into a highly spicy, sassy staple of Cajun cuisine. And an even spicier American link is Tex-Mex chorizo.

Big Bangers: The History of British Sausages

Sausages in Great Britain date back to at least the Roman occupation. In fact, archeological evidence suggests that the Romans built at least one sausage factory in a town called Verulamium, which today is St. Albans.

After the Romans returned to Rome in 410, the Angles, Saxons, and Normans left their imprint on what was to become British cuisine. The Anglo-Saxons and the Normans contributed to the stewing, roasting, and stuffing techniques, which of course influenced the development of sausages.

Sausage makers used the meat of hogs, beef, and sheep in their sausages. As in other regions of the world, people made meat into sausages to help preserve it. To make the meat go further, English sausage makers added breadcrumbs and oatmeal to sausages.

Both royals and common folk ate sausages, but royalty had more exacting standards. A cookbook from King Richard II calls for combining chicken and pork meat with grated bread, eggs, ginger, and saffron to form sausages. During Queen Elizabeth's time, raisins, dates, sugar, eggs, breadcrumbs, cloves, mace, and saffron were combined with pig livers. Queen Victoria had stringent guidelines for her sausages, requiring the meat to be chopped, not minced, and the casings to be filled by hand.

> **PRIME CUT**
>
> Scotland's national dish, haggis, is basically a sausage made of organ meats and oatmeal in a sheep's stomach. Scottish poet Robert Burns immortalized it in his poem *Address to a Haggis*.

Sausages that were developed in the British Isles were different from the sausages of mainland Europe. For one thing, fresh sausages became and to this day remain much more popular than smoked or cured sausages. In addition, bread and cereal fillings became and remain popular in sausage making.

Modern British Sausage Making

Modern British sausage making has its roots in the Victorian Age, when the very first sausage factories were built and were eventually replaced by the larger factories that exist today.

> **PRIME CUT**
>
> British sausages got their nickname—bangers—during World War II. Because of rationing and shortages, sausages made during the war contained a lot of water—so much so that they exploded with a bang during cooking.

The trend of larger companies buying out smaller firms continued after the war, but some smaller butchers managed to hang on. Today, more than 470 different kinds of sausage are made in Great Britain, and Great Britain holds the world's record for the world's longest sausage, which stretched 35 miles long and weighed 15.5 tons.

A Colony of Sausage Makers: American Sausages

English colonists brought sausages and sausage making to what is now the United States. But they weren't the first sausage makers, as Native Americans made sausage-like preserved meats such as pemmican.

These original colonists brought with them the tradition of breakfast sausage, which is very similar to the breakfast sausages served today throughout the United States.

But the English weren't the only ones who brought sausage making with them to "the New World." The French also brought their traditions, and in Louisiana, their culinary prowess mingled with Spanish and African traditions to create the Cajun and Creole cuisine we know today.

Other immigrants, especially those from Germany, Poland, and Italy, brought their sausage making traditions to the United States, too. In fact, German sausage making traditions evolved in Pennsylvania, Wisconsin, and Texas.

But of all the sausages that took root in American culture, perhaps none is as iconic as the hotdog. The American hotdog, in all of its variations, was adapted from either the German frankfurter, the Austrian wiener, or the Czech parkys, all of which are similarly styled sausages.

PRIME CUT

Hotdogs didn't truly emerge as populist, American fare until President Franklin D. Roosevelt and Eleanor Roosevelt publicly served them at a picnic to visiting King George VI and his wife.

Sausages continue to evolve, and one of the most exciting evolutions is the return to artisan sausage making. Today, more and more handcrafted sausages are appearing on restaurant menus, and corner butcher shops are reviving old traditions and starting new ones.

Oxford-Style Bangers

This sausage tastes like a cross between a bratwurst and a breakfast sausage. The eggs and breadcrumbs in the sausage give it a lighter texture.

Yield:	Prep time:	Cook time:	Serving size:
12 (5-ounce) links	60 minutes	30 minutes	1 link

2 TB. kosher salt

4 tsp. dried sage

4 tsp. lemon zest

1 tsp. ground black pepper

1 tsp. ground white pepper

½ tsp. ground nutmeg

½ tsp. ground mace

½ tsp. dried thyme

½ tsp. dried marjoram

4 lb. boneless pork shoulder, with no additional fat

4 large eggs

1 cup panko breadcrumbs or any unseasoned breadcrumbs

1 cup chicken broth or water, chilled

8 ft. hog casing or 32 mm collagen casing

1. In a small bowl, combine kosher salt, sage, lemon zest, black pepper, white pepper, nutmeg, mace, thyme, and marjoram. Set aside.

2. Cut pork into cubes for grinding and place in a large mixing bowl or hotel pan.

3. Using your hands or a wooden spoon, toss meat with spice mix until spices are evenly dispersed. Store in a covered container in the refrigerator or freezer until you're ready for the next step. Chill mixture for at least 30 minutes to improve grinding quality.

4. Grind mixture through a medium plate (see Chapter 4).

5. Add eggs, panko breadcrumbs, and chicken broth to ground meat. Using your hands or a tabletop mixer, mix until the texture is consistent, about 5 minutes.

6. Make a test patty, cook it, taste it, and adjust seasonings as necessary.

7. Chill mixture in a covered container in the refrigerator or freezer until you're ready for the next step.

8. Stuff mixture in hog or collagen casing (see Chapter 4).

CHEF'S CHOICE

Serve Oxford-Style Bangers with gravy and mashed potatoes for a traditional English meal of bangers and mash.

Cumberland-Style Bangers

This peppery English sausage has a light herbal nuance and boasts an extra richness from the addition of pork belly.

Yield:	Prep time:	Cook time:	Serving size:
12 (5-ounce) links	60 minutes	30 minutes	1 link

2 TB. kosher salt

2 tsp. ground black pepper

2 tsp. ground white pepper

¼ tsp. dried marjoram

¼ tsp. dried sage

⅛ tsp. ground cayenne

⅛ tsp. ground nutmeg

⅛ tsp. ground mace

2 lb. boneless pork shoulder with no additional fat

2 lb. pork belly

¾ cup panko breadcrumbs or any unseasoned breadcrumbs

⅔ cup ice water

8 ft. hog casing or 32 mm collagen casing

1. In a small bowl, combine kosher salt, black pepper, white pepper, marjoram, sage, cayenne, nutmeg, and mace. Set aside.

2. Cut pork shoulder and pork belly into cubes for grinding and place in a large mixing bowl or hotel pan.

3. Using your hands or a wooden spoon, toss meat with spice mix until spices are evenly dispersed. Store in a covered container in the refrigerator or freezer until you're ready for the next step. Chill mixture for at least 30 minutes to improve grinding quality.

4. Grind mixture through a medium plate (see Chapter 4).

5. Add panko breadcrumbs and ice water to ground meat. Using your hands or a tabletop mixer, mix until the texture is consistent, about 5 minutes.

6. Make a test patty, cook it, taste it, and adjust seasonings as necessary.

7. Chill mixture in a covered container in the refrigerator or freezer until you're ready for the next step.

8. Stuff mixture in hog or collagen casing (see Chapter 4).

PRIME CUT

The Cumberland sausage has been around for at least 500 years in the county of Cumberland in Great Britain. It traditionally is sold in one long coil up to 20 inches.

Cajun Boudin Blanc Sausage

This is a spicy Cajun sausage with bold pepper and garlic flavors and, of course, a lot of heat from the cayenne. This sausage has a unique texture because you cook the meat before grinding it, which gives it a finer, softer mouthfeel.

Yield:	Prep time:	Cook time:	Serving size:
18 (5-ounce) links	2 hours	30 minutes	1 link

2 TB. Spanish sweet paprika

1 TB. onion powder

1 TB. garlic powder

1 tsp. ground black pepper

$\frac{1}{2}$ tsp. ground white pepper

1 tsp. cayenne

4 lb. boneless pork shoulder with no additional fat

2 TB. kosher salt

1 qt. water

3 cups cooked medium-grain white rice

$\frac{1}{4}$ cup green onions, chopped

2 TB. parsley, chopped

Tabasco sauce or Louisiana-style hot sauce

8 ft. hog casing or 38 mm collagen casing

1. In a small bowl, combine Spanish sweet paprika, onion powder, garlic powder, black pepper, white pepper, and cayenne. Set aside.

2. Cut pork into cubes, put in a medium sauce pot, and add enough water to cover meat. Add 3 tablespoons spice mix and kosher salt.

3. Cook on medium-low heat for 1 hour or until fork tender. If the water level drops below meat, add more water.

4. When meat is tender, remove and drain meat, reserving cooking liquid. Allow meat and cooking liquid to cool to room temperature.

5. Grind mixture through a medium plate (see Chapter 4). Because the meat is cooked, it doesn't have to be chilled prior to grinding.

6. Add white rice, green onions, parsley, Tabasco sauce (to taste), and 2 cups of the cooking liquid to ground meat. Using your hands or a tabletop mixer, mix until the texture is consistent, about 5 minutes, adding up to 1 more cup cooking liquid if necessary. Taste mixture for seasoning and add more of the spice mix and/or kosher salt to taste.

7. Stuff mixture in hog or collagen casing (see Chapter 4).

8. Steam links for about 10 to 15 minutes before serving. Because the meat has already been cooked, just heat them through.

Variation: Instead of stuffing into links, bulk boudin can also be rolled into balls the size of golf balls and deep fried in 350°F peanut or vegetable oil. Fry until golden brown, about 7 minutes.

CHEF'S CHOICE

To make a Cajun spice blend to add to other dishes, simply mix Spanish sweet paprika, onion powder, garlic powder, black pepper, white pepper, and cayenne in the quantities listed in the ingredients list and store the mixture in a dry, airtight container. Add the spice blend to butter to create a Creole butter, toss with pasta to give it a kick, or sprinkle over popcorn.

All-American Hot Dogs

Meaty and fresh, this tastes like an upscale version of what you get at the ballpark.

Yield:	Prep time:	Cook time:	Serving size:
12 (5-ounce) links	60 minutes	30 minutes	1 link

4 tsp. kosher salt

1 tsp. cure powder #1

2 TB. dry yellow mustard

1 TB. paprika

1 tsp. ground black pepper

2 tsp. ground mace

1 tsp. garlic powder

1 tsp. ground coriander

½ tsp. ground celery seeds

5 lb. boneless beef chuck, with all visible fat removed

2 tsp. liquid smoke

1 cup ice water

20 ft. sheep casing or 24 mm hot dog collagen casing

1. In a small bowl, combine kosher salt, cure powder #1, dry yellow mustard, paprika, black pepper, mace, garlic powder, coriander, and celery seeds. Set aside.

2. Cut beef into cubes for grinding. Grind mixture through a fine plate twice (see Chapter 4). Store in a covered container in the refrigerator or freezer until you're ready for the next step.

3. Add spice mix and liquid smoke to ground meat and mix with your hands until spices are evenly dispersed. Store in a covered container in the refrigerator or freezer until you're ready for the next step.

4. In small batches, purée mixture in a food processor for about 3 minutes or until smooth, adding ice water in small amounts as needed. The consistency should be completely uniform when finished.

5. Mix together all batches in case there is any variation between batches.

6. Make a test patty, cook it, taste it, and adjust seasonings as necessary.

7. Chill mixture in a covered container in the refrigerator until you're ready for the next step.

8. Stuff mixture in natural or collagen casing (see Chapter 4). Refrigerate in a covered container for 2 hours to cure.

9. Place hot dogs in a large pot over medium-low heat and completely cover with water. Simmer in 200°F water until cooked through, about 30 minutes. Refrigerate hot dogs until you're ready to reheat and eat.

Variation: If you want to smoke the hot dogs to create a traditional frankfurter, omit liquid smoke and follow your smoker's instructions.

PRIME CUT

The average American eats 60 hot dogs a year, which is more than 1 each week.

Texas Chorizo

This sausage tastes like Tex-Mex cuisine in a casing. With four types of chilies, this hot and spicy link isn't for the faint of heart.

Yield:	Prep time:	Cook time:	Serving size:
2 pounds bulk or 6 (5-ounce) links	60 minutes	30 minutes	5 ounces bulk or 1 link

3 tsp. kosher salt

2 TB. Spanish hot paprika

1 cup onion, chopped

3 tsp. dried Ancho chilies, ground

1 tsp. dried Guajillo chilies, ground

1 tsp. dried Pasilla chilies, ground

2 chipotle chilies from can, finely chopped

2 tsp. adobo sauce from the canned chipotle chilies

1 tsp. garlic powder

1 tsp. ground cumin

$\frac{1}{2}$ tsp. ground black pepper

$\frac{1}{2}$ tsp. dried Mexican oregano

$\frac{1}{4}$ tsp. ground cayenne

$\frac{1}{4}$ tsp. ground coriander

2 lb. boneless pork shoulder with up to $\frac{1}{4}$ lb. additional fat

$\frac{1}{3}$ cup cider vinegar

2 tsp. liquid smoke

4 ft. hog casing or 32 mm collagen casing (optional)

1. In a medium bowl, combine kosher salt, Spanish hot paprika, onion, Ancho chilies, Guajillo chilies, Pasilla chilies, chipotle chilies, adobo sauce, garlic powder, cumin, black pepper, Mexican oregano, cayenne, and coriander. Set aside.

2. Cut pork into cubes for grinding and place in a large mixing bowl or hotel pan.

3. Using your hands or a wooden spoon, toss meat with spice mix until spices are evenly dispersed. Store in a covered container in the refrigerator or freezer until you're ready for the next step. Chill mixture for at least 30 minutes to improve grinding quality.

4. Grind mixture through a medium plate (see Chapter 4).

5. Add cider vinegar and liquid smoke to ground meat. Using your hands or a tabletop mixer, mix until the texture is consistent, about 5 minutes.

6. Make a test patty, cook it, taste it, and adjust seasonings as necessary.

7. Chill mixture in a covered container in the refrigerator or freezer until you're ready for the next step.

8. Stuff in hog or collagen casing (if using; see Chapter 4) or use as bulk sausage.

Exotic Sausage Recipes

After you understand the basics of making sausages, you can move on to making more exotic recipes. In these chapters, you find out how to make leaner sausages using poultry, seafood, and vegetables. Chapters in this part also show you how to make Asian sausages and game sausages.

Asian Sausages

In This Chapter

- Asia's sausage heritage
- Sausage recipes from Asia

Pigs were first domesticated in Asia, so it's only natural that the Asian continent has a long history of sausage making. As a matter of fact, Asian sausages are some of the most exotic and interesting sausages in the world. Some of them are spicy with Sichuan peppercorns, others sing with the flavors of ginger and lemongrass, and still others offer both sweet and savory notes. While they're great on their own, they also are quite delicious when added to stir-fries, eggrolls, and other dishes. This chapter introduces you to a sampling of these succulent links.

An Overview of Asia's Sausage Heritage

Though the earliest murals of sausage making were found in China, along with the first domesticated pigs, you won't find the breadth of sausage making in Asia that you do in Europe. Sausages in Asia, like Europe, developed out of necessity. People needed to use the whole pig and to preserve it.

The predominant style of sausage in Asia is lop cheong, which is a sweet sausage made with sugar, soy sauce, *five-spice powder*, and sweet rice wine. The sausage is then usually cured. Different versions of lop cheong can be found throughout China, as well as Thailand, Laos, and Vietnam.

Thai sausages sometimes have rice added as a filler, and they're usually highly spiced affairs, filled with lemongrass, fish sauce, curry, and Thai basil. The sausages in the Philippines combine Chinese and Spanish sausage making traditions to create their own distinct sausages.

Most traditional Asian sausages are made with pork, but sausage makers sometimes add duck, fish, and seafood as well.

Some of the more exotic ingredients in this chapter's recipes are not carried at your average grocery store. Whole Foods and Trader Joe's carry many of the ingredients, and spice stores typically carry five-spice powder and Sichuan peppercorns. But some of the best places to shop for these ingredients are Asian grocery stores, which stock all the more exotic ingredients called for in these recipes: the wines, vinegars, curry paste, and fish sauce, as well as fresh ingredients like ginger, galangal, and lemongrass. They also typically have great deals on ingredients such as rice, eggroll wrappers, and soy sauce. But be more cautious when purchasing meats from Asian markets, as sometimes they are of lesser quality.

Fresh Lop Cheong Chinese Sausage

This is an uncured version of the Sichuan-Style Cured Lop Cheong sausage recipe in Chapter 14. The sweet, aromatic flavors in this sausage are addictive.

Yield:	Prep time:	Cook time:	Serving size:
6 (5-ounce) links	60 minutes	30 minutes	1 link

1½ TB. kosher salt

4 TB. sugar

1 tsp. ground black pepper

1 tsp. five-spice powder

1 tsp. Sichuan peppercorns, crushed

4 lb. boneless pork shoulder with up to ½ lb. additional fat

¼ cup. light soy sauce

4 TB. Chinese rose wine or Shaoshing rice wine

8 ft. hog casing or 32 mm collagen casing

1. In a small bowl, combine kosher salt, sugar, black pepper, five-spice powder, and Sichuan peppercorns. Set aside.

2. Cut pork into cubes for grinding and place in a large mixing bowl or hotel pan.

3. Using your hands or a wooden spoon, toss meat with spice mix until spices are evenly dispersed. Store in a covered container in the refrigerator or freezer until you're ready for the next step. Chill mixture for at least 30 minutes to improve grinding quality.

4. Grind mixture through a medium plate (see Chapter 4).

5. Add soy sauce and Chinese rose wine to ground meat. Using your hands or a tabletop mixer, mix until the texture is consistent, about 5 minutes.

6. Make a test patty, cook it, taste it, and adjust seasonings as necessary.

7. Chill mixture in a covered container in the refrigerator or freezer until you're ready for the next step.

8. Stuff mixture in hog or collagen casing (see Chapter 4).

Variation: You can substitute cooking sherry if you can't find either Chinese rose wine or Shaoshing rice wine.

PRIME CUT

Lop Cheong is the most popular of all Asian sausages, and it's the go-to sausage for any dim sum (appetizers) recipes that call for sausage.

Fresh Issan Thai Sausage

This classic Thai sausage has rice in it, which acts as a filler and adds a different texture. The lime juice in the sausage adds an extra tanginess.

Yield:	Prep time:	Cook time:	Serving size:
12 (5-ounce) links	60 minutes	30 minutes	1 link

$1\frac{1}{2}$ TB. kosher salt

2 tsp. ground black pepper

2 tsp. ground white pepper

1 tsp. sugar

4 lb. boneless pork shoulder with up to $\frac{1}{2}$ lb. additional fat

$1\frac{1}{2}$ cup steamed sticky rice

5 tbs. garlic, finely chopped

1 tsp. lime zest (two limes)

1 cup lime juice (four limes)

2 TB. fish sauce

8 ft. hog casing or 32 mm collagen casing

1. In a small bowl, combine kosher salt, black pepper, white pepper, and sugar. Set aside.

2. Cut pork into cubes for grinding and place in a large mixing bowl or hotel pan.

3. Using your hands or a wooden spoon, toss meat with spice mix until spices are evenly dispersed. Store in a covered container in the refrigerator or freezer until you're ready for the next step. Chill mixture for at least 30 minutes to improve grinding quality.

4. Grind mixture through a fine or medium plate (see Chapter 4).

5. Add sticky rice, garlic, lime zest, lime juice, and fish sauce to ground meat. Using your hands or a tabletop mixer, mix ingredients until the texture is consistent, about 5 minutes.

6. Make a test patty, cook it, taste it, and adjust seasonings as necessary.

7. Chill mixture in a covered container in the refrigerator or freezer until you're ready for the next step.

8. Stuff mixture in hog or collagen casing (see Chapter 4).

9. This sausage is traditionally steamed for about 30 minutes, but can then be used in a stir-fry or browned to enhance the flavor. To brown the sausage, heat about 2 teaspoons vegetable or peanut oil in a large sauté pan on medium-high heat. Add cooked sausage to the pan and brown on all sides, about 4 minutes on each side.

> **PRIME CUT**
>
> Fish sauce is a traditional Thai ingredient used in many Thai dishes. It smells and tastes awful on its own, but when used in moderation, it greatly enhances the savory flavors of many dishes.

Sai Oua Thai Sausage

This sausage has all the flavor of a Thai red curry. It is very aromatic and quite spicy.

Yield:	Prep time:	Cook time:	Serving size:
12 (5-ounce) links	60 minutes	30 minutes	1 link

6 TB. lemongrass, roughly chopped

4 TB. *galangal* (also called galanga, blue ginger, or lao), peeled and roughly chopped, or chopped fresh ginger

2 medium shallots, peeled

4 cloves garlic, peeled

2 TB. Thai chili peppers, finely chopped, with or without seeds (optional)

1½ TB. kosher salt

2 tsp. ground black pepper

4 lb. boneless pork shoulder with up to ½ lb. additional fat

1 cup cilantro, finely chopped

4 TB. red curry paste

1 tsp. lime zest (about 2 limes), finely chopped

¾ cup lime juice (about 3 limes)

1 TB. fish sauce

8 ft. hog casing or 32 mm collagen casing

1. Put lemongrass and galangal in a food processor and process until they are very finely chopped. Add shallots and garlic and run until finely chopped. Add Thai chili peppers (if using), kosher salt, and black pepper and repeat. Set aside.

2. Cut pork into cubes for grinding and place in a large mixing bowl or hotel pan.

3. Using your hands or a wooden spoon, toss meat with lemongrass mixture until it is evenly dispersed. Store in a covered container in the refrigerator or freezer until you're ready for the next step. Chill mixture for at least 30 minutes to improve grinding quality.

4. Grind mixture through a fine or medium plate (see Chapter 4).

5. Add cilantro, red curry paste, lime zest, lime juice, and fish sauce to ground meat. Using your hands or a tabletop mixer, mix until the texture is consistent, about 5 minutes.

6. Make a test patty, cook it, taste it, and adjust seasonings as necessary.

7. Chill mixture in a covered container in the refrigerator or freezer until you're ready for the next step.

8. Stuff mixture in hog or collagen casing (see Chapter 4).

Variation: As this already tastes like a great Thai curry, why not add this to your curry instead of chicken or beef?

DEFINITION

Galangal is a root in the ginger family, but it has a completely different taste. It's more peppery than ginger, with almost a floral and citrusy aroma. By itself, it's pretty pungent, but it adds great depth to many dishes, including curries and soups.

Fresh Goon Chiang Thai Sausage

This is a "mock cure," semi-cooked version of a popular sweet dried Thai sausage. By making it this way, you can avoid the use of nitrites and nitrates.

Yield:	Prep time:	Cook time:	Serving size:
6 (5-ounce) links	60 minutes	30 minutes	1 link

1½ TB. kosher salt

1 tsp. ground black pepper

⅓ cup. sugar

4 lb. boneless pork shoulder with up to ½ lb. additional fat

¾ cup white rice wine

¼ cup soy sauce

8 ft. hog casing or 32 mm collagen casing

1. In a small bowl, combine kosher salt, black pepper, and sugar. Set aside.

2. Cut pork into cubes for grinding and place in a large mixing bowl or hotel pan.

3. Using your hands or a wooden spoon, toss meat with spice mix until spices are evenly dispersed. Store in a covered container in the refrigerator or freezer until you're ready for the next step. Chill mixture for at least 30 minutes to improve grinding quality.

4. Grind mixture through a fine or medium plate (see Chapter 4).

5. Add white rice wine and soy sauce to ground meat. Using your hands or a table-top mixer, mix until the texture is consistent, about 5 minutes.

6. Make a test patty, cook it, taste it, and adjust seasonings as necessary.

7. Chill mixture in a covered container in the refrigerator or freezer until you're ready for the next step.

8. Stuff mixture in hog or collagen casing (see Chapter 4) and make large links (8 to 12 inches).

9. Place links on two baking sheets lined with parchment paper and dry in a 175°F oven for 3 to 4 hours. After 1½ hours, flip sausages and switch order of the pans in the oven to ensure even drying.

CHEF'S CHOICE

This sausage is often tossed into salads. Try adding it to salads made of greens, cucumbers, carrots, red onions, and radishes, and toss it with a ginger dressing.

Longanisa Filipino Sausage

This sausage is almost like sweet Italian sausage with a slightly spicy ginger twist.

Yield:	Prep time:	Cook time:	Serving size:
6 (5-ounce) links	60 minutes	30 minutes	1 link

2½ TB. kosher salt

⅓ cup white sugar

1 tsp. ground ginger

½ tsp. ground black pepper

½ tsp. ground white pepper

2 TB. garlic, finely chopped

1 tsp. red pepper flakes

6 lb. boneless pork shoulder with up to ⅔ lb. additional fat

½ cup Sukang Iloco or other Filipino vinegar

8 ft. hog casing or 32 mm collagen casing

1. In a small bowl, combine kosher salt, white sugar, ginger, black pepper, white pepper, garlic, and red pepper flakes. Set aside.

2. Cut pork into cubes for grinding and place in a large mixing bowl or hotel pan.

3. Using your hands or a wooden spoon, toss meat with spice mix until spices are evenly dispersed. Store in a covered container in the refrigerator or freezer until you're ready for the next step. Chill mixture for at least 30 minutes to improve grinding quality.

4. Grind mixture through a medium plate (see Chapter 4).

5. Add Sukang Iloco vinegar to ground meat. Using your hands or a tabletop mixer, mix until the texture is consistent, about 5 minutes.

6. Make a test patty, cook it, taste it, and adjust seasoning as necessary.

7. Chill mixture in a covered container in the refrigerator or freezer until you're ready for the next step.

8. Stuff mixture in hog or collagen casing (see Chapter 4).

Variation: You can substitute distilled white vinegar for the Sukang Iloco vinegar.

CHEF'S CHOICE

Some versions of this sausage have rum and brown sugar added. Simply substitute the white sugar for brown sugar and add a tablespoon or two of rum.

Poultry, Seafood, and Vegetarian Sausages

In This Chapter

- Poultry sausages
- Seafood sausages
- Vegetarian sausages
- Poultry, seafood, and vegetarian sausage recipes

Lean and *healthy* aren't often the words used to describe sausages, but both of these adjectives are accurate labels for the sausages in this chapter. While the majority of the world's sausages have traditionally been made with pork and/or beef, you can make some particularly tasty sausages with poultry, seafood, and even vegetables.

Besides their lower fat content, these ingredients have a milder taste, offering sausage chefs more of a blank canvas in which to impart a greater variety of flavors. This chapter explores the advantages of leaner meats and how you can use vegetables, tofu, and grains to create sausages, too.

How Poultry Sausages Evolved

Historically, sausages were made to help preserve a whole butchered animal. Since a whole chicken can be eaten within a day or two, there was no need to preserve its meat.

But while poultry meat wasn't added to sausages to preserve it, butchers did sometimes add it to sausages to impart a particular flavor or texture. This was especially true in France, where *boudin blanc*, a highly seasoned sausage, often combined pork with chicken. Other sausages in France also were made with duck and goose meat, too.

The British also occasionally made sausages by combining pork with chicken. One cookbook for Richard II calls for boiling hens and pork together before combining them with breadcrumbs in a sausage.

You can take just about any sausage recipe and replace the pork and beef with chicken or turkey. But because they are leaner meats, you may need to use additional water or liquid so that they don't dry out. In addition, because poultry is generally milder than pork or beef, garnishes help poultry sausages sing. Fresh herbs, fruits and vegetables all taste great in poultry sausages. Poultry sausages also taste great when wines—white wines unless you want them to turn purple or gray—are incorporated.

Poultry's mild nature also means that certain sausage recipes might not lend themselves as naturally to substituting poultry for other meats like pork or beef. Chorizos, for example, are tricky territory—their intense flavors of cumin, paprika, and chile blast right through poultry meat. Similarly, game sausages, because of their strong meat flavor, don't lend themselves to poultry substitutions.

For leaner poultry versions of intense sausages, you might want to try combining half pork and half chicken, then adjust the spices accordingly. But if you still have your heart set on a pure Colombian chicken chorizo, for example, make a small test batch to see how the flavors work. Then, you can make adjustments.

A Bit About Seafood Sausages

Coastal regions traditionally have had some type of seafood sausages. France, for example, has had some delectable seafood sausages, including a seafood choucroute, made with smoked fish and sauerkraut, and other sausages made with shrimp and lobster, too. Great Britain has also had some seafood sausages, particularly oyster sausages.

Although you can certainly substitute seafood and fish for pork or beef in your sausages, we don't recommend doing so. Different seafoods and fish have particular flavor profiles, and they're even leaner than poultry. A fish bratwurst, for example, won't taste anything like a traditional bratwurst.

To best experiment with creating new seafood sausages, examine the spice and herb profiles you prefer to match with seafoods, and then test them. You can also experiment by adding a bit of seafood—shrimp, for example—as a garnish in some sausage recipes.

When cooking seafood sausages, poach them on a lower temperature and avoid using a highly seasoned poaching liquid, as you don't want to overwhelm the delicate flavors of the sausage.

Vegetarian Sausages

Traditionally, sausages have always been made with meat, or at least fat or suet, as an ingredient. But with a growing interest in both vegetarian and healthier eating, vegetarian sausages have become more popular.

> **PRIME CUT**
>
> Though it would seem that vegan sausages are a late twentieth-century creation, the first soy sausages were actually invented in 1916 in Germany.

Most vegetarian sausages are made commercially by large factories, but you can make even healthier versions at home. You can use tofu and other soy proteins as well as vegetables, fruit, nuts, beans, and grains.

Instead of grinding the meat substitute in a meat grinder, you may want to just pulse them in a food processor. You will need to add some binders like egg, milk, or oil. Vegetarian sausages, especially those made from soy, are pretty mild in flavor, so you'll need to add fresh herbs and spices.

There are no non-animal-based sausage casings available on the market at this time. Unlike commercially made veggie sausages—in which ingredients are pressure treated to form links—you'll have to form your links by hand, using corn husks, banana leaves, and other wraps. You can also use aluminum foil, which is perhaps the most versatile and user-friendly method.

Because they are milder than meat sausages, if you wish to create a "vegetarian bratwurst," for example, cut the seasonings in half, and do a test batch.

Vegetarian sausages also typically require shorter cooking times.

Apple Chicken Sausage

The sweetness of apples brings out the inherent sweetness of the meat. This mild sausage is delicious both as a breakfast or dinner sausage.

Yield:	Prep time:	Cook time:	Serving size:
6 (5-ounce) links	60 minutes	30 minutes	1 link

1 tsp. kosher salt

1 tsp. poultry seasoning

½ tsp. ground black pepper

¼ tsp. sage

¼ tsp. chopped rosemary

1 pinch ground nutmeg

2 lb. boneless chicken breast

3 egg whites

½ cup panko breadcrumbs

1 cup peeled and cored apples, finely diced

4 ft. hog casing or 32 mm collagen casing (optional)

1. In a small bowl, combine kosher salt, poultry seasoning, black pepper, sage, rosemary, and nutmeg. Set aside.

2. Cut chicken into cubes for grinding and place in a large mixing bowl or hotel pan.

3. Using your hands or a wooden spoon, toss meat with spice mix until spices are evenly dispersed. Store in a covered container in the refrigerator or freezer until you're ready for the next step. Chill mixture for at least 30 minutes to improve grinding quality.

4. Grind mixture through a medium plate (see Chapter 4).

5. Add egg whites, panko breadcrumbs, and apples to ground meat. Using your hands or a tabletop mixer, mix until the texture is consistent, about 5 minutes.

6. Make a test patty, cook it, taste it, and adjust seasonings as necessary.

7. Chill mixture in a covered container in the refrigerator or freezer until you're ready for the next step.

8. Stuff mixture in hog or collagen casing (if using; see Chapter 4) or use as bulk sausage.

CHEF'S CHOICE

This is a great sausage for breakfast sandwiches. Simply form the sausage into patties instead of links.

Chicken and Basil Sausage

The clean, crisp, almost minty taste of basil sings through in this sausage.

Yield:	Prep time:	Cook time:	Serving size:
6 (5-ounce) links	60 minutes	30 minutes	1 link

1 tsp. kosher salt

3 TB. chopped fresh basil

¼ tsp. ground black pepper

¼ tsp. ground white pepper

¼ tsp. ground cloves

⅛ tsp. dried thyme

⅛ tsp. dried marjoram

⅛ tsp. dried mint

2 lb. boneless chicken breast

¼ cup heavy cream

3 egg whites

2 tsp. sherry vinegar

½ cup panko breadcrumbs

4 ft. hog casing or 32 mm collagen casing

1. In a small bowl, combine kosher salt, basil, black pepper, white pepper, cloves, thyme, marjoram, and mint. Set aside.

2. Cut chicken into cubes for grinding and place in a large mixing bowl or hotel pan.

3. Using your hands or a wooden spoon, toss chicken with spice mix until spices are evenly dispersed. Store in a covered container in the refrigerator or freezer until you're ready for the next step. Chill mixture for at least 30 minutes to improve grinding quality.

4. Grind mixture through a medium plate (see Chapter 4).

5. Add heavy cream, egg whites, sherry vinegar, and panko breadcrumbs to ground meat. Using your hands or a tabletop mixer, mix until the texture is consistent, about 5 minutes.

6. Make a test patty, cook it, taste it, and adjust seasonings as necessary.

7. Chill mixture in a covered container in the refrigerator or freezer until you're ready for the next step.

8. Stuff mixture in hog or collagen casing (see Chapter 4).

CHEF'S CHOICE

Chicken and basil sausage is a great addition to Italian dishes. It's also a great base recipe in which to try out different herbs.

Turkey Brats

If you're a big fan of bratwurst, but prefer to lighten the calories, this is the sausage for you. It tastes just like a brat, only a bit leaner.

Yield:	Prep time:	Cook time:	Serving size:
6 (5-ounce) links	60 minutes	30 minutes	1 link

1 tsp. kosher salt

1 TB. ground sage

1 tsp. ground white pepper

1 tsp. ground black pepper

¼ tsp. ground allspice

¼ tsp. ground mace

2 lb. boneless turkey breast

¼ cup heavy cream

4 ft. hog casing or 32 mm collagen casing (optional)

1. In a small bowl, combine kosher salt, sage, white pepper, black pepper, allspice, and mace. Set aside.

2. Cut turkey into cubes for grinding and place in a large mixing bowl or hotel pan.

3. Using your hands or a wooden spoon, toss turkey with spice mix until spices are evenly dispersed. Store in a covered container in the refrigerator or freezer until you're ready for the next step. Chill mixture for at least 30 minutes to improve grinding quality.

4. Grind mixture through a medium plate (see Chapter 4).

5. Add heavy cream to ground meat. Using your hands or a tabletop mixer, mix until the texture is consistent, about 5 minutes.

6. Make a test patty, cook it, taste it, and adjust seasonings as necessary.

7. Chill mixture in a covered container in the refrigerator or freezer until you're ready for the next step.

8. Stuff mixture in hog or collagen casing (if using; see Chapter 4) or use as bulk sausage.

PRIME CUT

The bratwurst was first popularized in Sheboygan, Wisconsin. Not coincidentally, Milwaukee's Miller Park Baseball Stadium (about an hour south of Sheboygan) is the only Major League park to sell more brats than hotdogs.

Fresh Turkey Kielbasa

This is a traditional kielbasa with a mild, garlicky flavor.

Yield:	Prep time:	Cook time:	Serving size:
12 (5-ounce) links	60 minutes	30 minutes	1 link

2 tsp. kosher salt

2 tsp. mustard seed, crushed

1 tsp. garlic powder

¾ tsp. ground black pepper

¼ tsp. ground allspice

¼ tsp. ground celery seed

4 lb. boneless turkey breast

½ cup heavy cream

8 ft. hog casing or 32 mm collagen casing

1. In a small bowl, combine kosher salt, mustard seed, garlic powder, black pepper, allspice, and celery seed. Set aside.

2. Cut turkey into cubes for grinding and place in a large mixing bowl or hotel pan.

3. Using your hands or a wooden spoon, toss turkey with spice mix until spices are evenly dispersed. Store in a covered container in the refrigerator or freezer until you're ready for the next step. Chill mixture for at least 30 minutes to improve grinding quality.

4. Grind mixture through a fine or medium plate (see Chapter 4).

5. Add heavy cream to ground meat. Using your hands or a tabletop mixer, mix until the texture is consistent, about 5 minutes.

6. Make a test patty, cook it, taste it, and adjust seasonings as necessary.

7. Chill mixture in a covered container in the refrigerator or freezer.

8. Stuff mixture in hog or collagen casing (see Chapter 4).

CHEF'S CHOICE

Turkey kielbasa can be used interchangeably with pork kielbasa in any recipe.

Turkey Italian Sausage

Zesty with oregano, garlic, and fennel, this light sausage has enough zip to make you think it has more calories than it does.

Yield:	Prep time:	Cook time:	Serving size:
15 (5-ounce) links	60 minutes	30 minutes	1 link

1 tsp. kosher salt

2 tsp. crushed fennel seed

1 tsp. garlic powder

½ tsp. dried oregano

½ tsp. ground black pepper

½ tsp. paprika

¼ tsp. dried basil

2 lb. boneless turkey breast

¼ cup ice water

4 ft. hog casing or 32 mm collagen casing (optional)

1. In a small bowl, combine kosher salt, fennel seed, garlic powder, oregano, black pepper, paprika, and basil. Set aside.

2. Cut turkey into cubes for grinding and place in a large mixing bowl or hotel pan.

3. Using your hands or a wooden spoon, toss turkey with spice mix until spices are evenly dispersed. Store in a covered container in the refrigerator or freezer until you're ready for the next step. Chill mixture for at least 30 minutes to improve grinding quality.

4. Grind mixture through a medium plate (see Chapter 4).

5. Add ice water to ground meat. Using your hands or a tabletop mixer, mix until the texture is consistent, about 5 minutes.

6. Make a test patty, cook it, taste it, and adjust seasoning as necessary.

7. Chill mixture in a covered container in the refrigerator or freezer until you're ready for the next step.

8. Stuff mixture in hog or collagen casing (if using; see Chapter 4) or use as bulk sausage.

CHEF'S CHOICE

Italian sausage isn't just great to add to Italian dishes. It also makes an amazing meatloaf, and it's also good for a mild chili.

Thai Chicken or Turkey Sausage

Sweet and spicy, this sausage packs a lot of flavor, and it sings with fresh herbs.

Yield:	Prep time:	Cook time:	Serving size:
6 (5-ounce) links	60 minutes	30 minutes	1 link

½ tsp. kosher salt

2 tsp. garlic, finely chopped

1 tsp. ground black pepper

¼ tsp. dried ginger

1 tsp. palm or table sugar

2 lb. boneless chicken or turkey breast

3 TB. cilantro, chopped

3 TB. Thai basil, chopped

1 TB. green or red curry paste

2 tsp. fish sauce

4 ft. hog casing or 32 mm collagen casing (optional)

1. In a small bowl, combine kosher salt, garlic, black pepper, ginger, and palm sugar. Set aside.

2. Cut chicken into cubes for grinding and place in a large mixing bowl or hotel pan.

3. Using your hands or a wooden spoon, toss chicken with spice mix until spices are evenly dispersed. Store in a covered container in the refrigerator or freezer until you're ready for the next step. Chill mixture for at least 30 minutes to improve grinding quality.

4. Grind mixture through a medium plate (see Chapter 4).

5. Add cilantro, Thai basil, green curry paste, and fish sauce to ground meat. Using your hands or a tabletop mixer, mix until the texture is consistent, about 5 minutes.

6. Make a test patty, cook it, taste it, and adjust seasonings as necessary.

7. Chill mixture in a covered container in the refrigerator or freezer until you're ready for the next step.

8. Stuff mixture in hog or collagen casing (if using; see Chapter 4) or use as bulk sausage.

PRIME CUT

Thai basil is different from sweet basil. Its leaves grow on a purple stem, and it has a bit of a licorice or anise taste to it. It tastes more like mint than sweet basil.

Duck Sausage

This very French sausage is moderately spiced with rosemary and thyme.

Yield:	Prep time:	Cook time:	Serving size:
12 (5-ounce) links	60 minutes	30 minutes	1 link

3 TB. kosher salt

1 tsp. ground black pepper

2 tsp. dried sage

1 tsp. dried thyme

1 tsp. dried rosemary, crushed

1 TB. garlic, finely chopped

1 TB. shallots, chopped

4 lb. boneless duck breast

1 lb. pork fat

½ TB. honey

¾ cup water

10 ft. hog casing or 32 mm collagen casing

1. In a small bowl, combine kosher salt, black pepper, sage, thyme, rosemary, garlic, and shallots. Set aside.

2. Cut duck and pork fat into cubes for grinding and place in a large mixing bowl or hotel pan.

3. Using your hands or a wooden spoon, toss meat with spice mix until spices are evenly dispersed. Store in a covered container in the refrigerator or freezer until you're ready for the next step. Chill mixture for at least 30 minutes to improve grinding quality.

4. Grind mixture through a medium plate (see Chapter 4).

5. Add honey and water to ground meat. Using your hands or a tabletop mixer, mix until the texture is consistent, about 5 minutes.

6. Make a test patty, cook it, taste it, and adjust seasonings as necessary.

7. Chill mixture in a covered container in the refrigerator or freezer until you're ready for the next step.

8. Stuff mixture in hog or collagen casing (see Chapter 4).

CHEF'S CHOICE

This sausage is ideal for smoking: simply reduce the salt to 2 tablespoons and add 1 teaspoon cure powder #1. Follow the smoking instructions in Chapter 14.

Seafood Boudin Sausage

The texture of this sausage is unusual, as it's bound with rice inside the casing. Light and fresh tasting with parsley and green onions, this is almost like a seafood risotto inside a link.

Yield:	Prep time:	Cook time:	Serving size:
20 (5-ounce) links	60 minutes	30 minutes	1 link

2 tsp. kosher salt

1 tsp. cayenne

$\frac{1}{2}$ tsp. white pepper

2 lb. crawfish tail meat, coarsely chopped

2 lb. shrimp, peeled and deveined, coarsely chopped

2 medium shallots, finely chopped

2 cloves garlic, finely chopped

3 TB. parsley, finely chopped

4 green onions, only green portion, finely chopped

5 cups cooked medium-grain rice

$\frac{1}{2}$ cup heavy cream

8 ft. hog casing or 38 mm collagen casing

1. In a large bowl or hotel pan, combine kosher salt, cayenne, and white pepper.

2. Add crawfish and shrimp to spice mix. Using your hands or a wooden spoon, toss seafood with spice mix until spices are evenly dispersed.

3. Add shallots, garlic, parsley, and green onions to mixture. Mix thoroughly with a wooden spoon or your hands.

4. Add rice and heavy cream and mix until all ingredients are evenly dispersed. Store in a covered container in the refrigerator until you're ready for the next step.

5. Stuff mixture in hog or collagen casing (see Chapter 4).

CHEF'S CHOICE

To prepare this delicate sausage, poach it on low heat for 10 to 15 minutes, or until cooked through. Serve it over a bed of Cajun dirty rice for a lovely meal.

Mixed Seafood Sausage

This contemporary American sausage is creamy with the, fresh taste of seafood.

Yield:	Prep time:	Cook time:	Serving size:
30 (5-ounce) links	60 minutes	30 minutes	1 link

2 tsp. kosher salt

2 TB. Old Bay seasoning

1½ lb. sole fillet, or other white fish

1½ lb. sea scallops, muscle tab (foot) removed

¾ cup panko breadcrumbs

2 cups heavy cream

3 eggs

¾ lb. shrimp, cut into ¼-inch dice

¾ lb. crab or lobster, cut into ¼-inch dice

½ lb. salmon, cut into ¼-inch dice

12 ft. hog casing or 32 mm collagen casing

1. In a small bowl, combine kosher salt and Old Bay seasoning. Set aside.

2. Cut sole and sea scallops into cubes for grinding and place in a large mixing bowl or hotel pan.

3. Using your hands or a wooden spoon, toss seafood with spice mix until spices are evenly dispersed. Store in a covered container in the refrigerator or freezer until you're ready for the next step. Chill mixture for at least 30 minutes to improve grinding quality.

4. Grind mixture through a fine plate (see Chapter 4).

5. In a medium bowl, soak panko breadcrumbs in 1 cup heavy cream and set aside.

6. In small batches, purée seafood mixture in a food processor for 1 minute per batch or until smooth, adding remaining 1 cup heavy cream in small amounts.

7. Add soaked breadcrumbs and eggs to seafood mixture and toss with a wooden spoon or your hands for 5 minutes or until the texture is consistent. Fold in diced shrimp, crab, and salmon. Chill mixture in a covered container in the refrigerator or freezer until you're ready for the next step.

8. Stuff mixture in hog or collagen casing (see Chapter 4).

9. Because sausage is delicate, poach it in lightly simmering water or white wine until cooked through, about 15 to 20 minutes, and then lightly sauté it.

Vegan Bean Sausage

This German-styled vegan sausage has hints of nutmeg and mace, but the spices don't overwhelm the sausage.

Yield:	Prep time:	Cook time:	Serving size:
4 (5-ounce) links	60 minutes	30 minutes	1 link

2 cups canned beans such as pinto or cannellini, rinsed and drained

½ cup whole-wheat breadcrumbs

⅓ cup vegetable stock

2 TB. extra-virgin olive oil

1 tsp. liquid smoke (or to taste)

1 tsp. dried thyme

½ tsp. garlic powder

¼ tsp. ground black pepper

⅛ tsp. ground dried ginger

⅛ tsp. ground allspice

⅛ tsp. ground mace

¼ tsp. red pepper flakes (optional)

1. In a medium bowl, mash beans into a rough paste with the back of a fork until no beans remain whole.

2. Add whole-wheat breadcrumbs, vegetable stock, extra-virgin olive oil, liquid smoke, thyme, garlic powder, black pepper, ginger, allspice, mace, and red pepper flakes (if using) and mix with a wooden spoon until combined.

3. Divide mixture into four or more portions. Place each portion on a sheet of foil. Roll the foil neatly around mixture to form links and twist the ends of the foil.

4. To cook, place links in a hot steamer and steam on medium heat for 30 to 40 minutes or until firm and cooked through.

5. When cooked, remove sausages from the steamer and allow to cool. Remove the foil and serve or store for later use.

Variation: If you prefer spicier sausages, increase the spices by 50 percent.

PRIME CUT

You can stuff the ingredients into a collagen casing, but because the casing is made from meat, the sausages will no longer be vegetarian.

Vegetarian Bulgur Sausage

This is a sweet, heavily herbed vegetarian sausage.

Yield:	Prep time:	Cook time:	Serving size:
4 (5-ounce) links	60 minutes	30 minutes	1 link

½ cup whole-wheat flour

2 cups cooked bulgur wheat

1 egg

¼ tsp. sea salt (or to taste)

1 large clove garlic, chopped

1 small shallot, chopped

¼ tsp. ground black pepper

¼ tsp. paprika

¼ tsp. ground coriander

¼ tsp. dried thyme

¼ tsp. dried rosemary

⅛ tsp. red pepper (or to taste)

½ TB. honey (or to taste)

1. In a medium bowl, combine ¼ cup whole-wheat flour, bulgur wheat, egg, sea salt, garlic, shallot, black pepper, paprika, coriander, thyme, rosemary, red pepper, and honey. Mix with a wooden spoon for 3 to 5 minutes or until texture is consistent.

   To fry sausages, proceed to step 2. To steam them, skip to step 3.

2. Divide mixture into four portions and roll into logs. Dredge sausages in remaining ¼ cup whole-wheat flour. Add canola or olive oil to a medium skillet over medium to medium-high heat and fry sausages for 10 to 12 minutes or until lightly browned and cooked through.

3. Alternatively, divide sausage mixture into four or more portions. Place each portion on a sheet of foil. Roll the foil neatly around the mixture to form links and twist the ends of the foil.

4. Place links in a hot steamer and steam on medium heat for 20 to 30 minutes or until firm and cooked through.

5. When cooked, remove sausages from the steamer and allow to cool. Remove foil and serve immediately, or store for later use.

Variation: To make this *vegan*, use a vegan egg replacement powder.

   DEFINITION

A **vegan** diet doesn't include any animal products whatsoever, including eggs, dairy, and, of course, meat.

Game Sausages

Chapter

13

In This Chapter

- Tips for making great game sausages
- Game sausage recipes

Game sausages are some of the most intensely flavored sausages you can make. You can choose from among a great variety of game meats, and you can make some amazing sausages from them. However, because game meat can sometimes be too intense and gamey, you need to take some precautions when preparing sausages from the meat of wild animals.

You've Got Game: Sausages from the Wild

Game meats have been used for centuries in sausage making. Royalty in both Poland and Great Britain were fond of hunting, and they loved to have their prey turned into tasty links. They weren't so different from today's hunters, who often have their bounty butchered into sausages.

Game sausages can be made with any sort of meat that people hunt or trap, including rabbit, squirrel, pheasant, deer, antelope, moose, and bear. With any of these meats, you're going to deal with gaminess. On the gamey spectrum, rabbits fall on the mild side, deer are in the middle, and bear are intense.

The bottom line, though, is that game meat tends to be very lean but potently flavored. To dial down the gaminess so that it's more palatable, keep the following points in mind.

- **The fat is gamier than the meat.** Remove all the visible fat as well as any tendons, collagen, or stringy bits. Replace the fat you remove with pork fat.

- **Increase the amount of spices to match the more intense flavor of the meat.** Traditional game sausage spices include garlic, onions, red peppers, and/or cayenne. Some also include juniper berries.

CHEF'S CHOICE

Juniper berries are a traditional ingredient in game sausages, especially French game sausages. Juniper berries give gin its ginny taste. Though it gives the same flavor to sausage, it's more subtle, and this flavor helps to cut the gamey taste.

Taming the Game with Pork

You can tone down the gaminess even further by adding some pork to the grind. A sausage made entirely of game meat might be a little too intense for the typical palate, and none of the recipes in this chapter calls for 100 percent game meat.

The basic guideline is to use a ratio of $1/3$ pork to $2/3$ game in your recipes, but you can increase the ratio of pork to $2/3$ to further reduce the gaminess. Since game sausage is all about highlighting the game meat, don't use any less than $1/3$ game meat unless you just want to add a taste of game to a pork sausage recipe.

If you're adapting a pork recipe to make a game sausage version, stick to the $1/3$ game to $2/3$ pork ratio, and increase the spices a little bit to match the more intense flavors of the game meat.

THE GRIND

If you process your game meat yourself, make sure the meat isn't full of buckshot or metal fragments. You also want to make sure that you remove the tendons, collagen, and stringy bits, as well as the fat.

Venison Italian Sausage

This is a gamey version of a traditional Italian sausage, with just the right amount of heat. This sausage is great for smoking (see Chapter 14).

Yield:	Prep time:	Cook time:	Serving size:
12 (5-ounce) links	60 minutes	30 minutes	1 link

2 TB. kosher salt

1 TB. sugar

2 TB. ground black pepper

2 TB. fennel, whole or cracked

1 TB. sweet Spanish paprika

1 tsp. garlic powder

1 tsp. red pepper flakes

½ tsp. cayenne pepper

2 lb. lean venison meat

2 lb. boneless pork shoulder with up to ¾ lb. additional fat

⅔ cup Italian red wine, such as Chianti

8 ft. hog casing or 32 mm collagen casing

1. In a small bowl, combine kosher salt, sugar, black pepper, fennel, sweet Spanish paprika, garlic powder, red pepper flakes, and cayenne pepper. Set aside.

2. Cut venison and pork into cubes for grinding and place in a large bowl.

3. Using your hands or a wooden spoon, toss meat with spice mix until spices are evenly dispersed. Store in a covered container in the refrigerator or freezer until you're ready for the next step. Chill mixture for at least 30 minutes to improve grinding quality.

4. Grind mixture through a medium plate (see Chapter 4).

5. Add Italian red wine to ground meat. Using your hands or a tabletop mixer, mix until the texture is consistent, about 5 minutes.

6. Make a test patty, cook it, taste it, and adjust seasonings as necessary.

7. Chill mixture in a covered container in the refrigerator or freezer until you're ready for the next step.

8. Stuff mixture in hog or collagen casing (see Chapter 4).

CHEF'S CHOICE

The hot spices in this recipe complement the venison quite well, but if you prefer a milder-tasting sausage, increase the ratio of pork.

Mild Venison Sausage

The venison in this sausage is complemented by garlic and black pepper.

Yield:	Prep time:	Cook time:	Serving size:
30 (5-ounce) links	60 minutes	30 minutes	1 link

5 TB. kosher salt

2 TB. ground black pepper

2 TB. granulated onion

2 TB. garlic powder

1 tsp. sugar

1 tsp. ground allspice

1 tsp. sweet Spanish paprika

1 tsp. sage

1 tsp. yellow mustard seed, crushed

7 lb. lean venison meat

3 lb. boneless pork shoulder with up to 1½ lb. additional fat

2 TB. liquid smoke

1⅓ cup cold water

20 ft. hog casing or 32 mm collagen casing

1. In a small bowl, combine kosher salt, black pepper, granulated onion, garlic powder, sugar, allspice, sweet Spanish paprika, sage, and yellow mustard seed. Set aside.

2. Cut venison and pork into cubes for grinding and place in a large bowl.

3. Using your hands or a wooden spoon, toss meat with spice mix until spices are evenly dispersed. Store in a covered container in the refrigerator or freezer until you're ready for the next step. Chill mixture for at least 30 minutes to improve grinding quality.

4. Grind mixture through a fine or medium plate (see Chapter 4).

5. Add liquid smoke and cold water to ground meat. Using your hands or a table-top mixer, mix until the texture is consistent, about 5 minutes.

6. Make a test patty, cook it, taste it, and adjust seasoning as necessary.

7. Chill mixture in a covered container in the refrigerator or freezer until you're ready for the next step.

8. Stuff mixture in hog or collagen casing (see Chapter 4).

CHEF'S CHOICE

If you want a hot venison sausage, simply increase the black pepper to 3 tablespoons and add 2 teaspoons red pepper flakes and 1 teaspoon cayenne.

Elk Sausage

The caraway, coriander, and mace give this game sausage a nice fragrant aroma, reminiscent of German sausages such as Thüringer or Nürnberg brats.

Yield:	Prep time:	Cook time:	Serving size:
30 (5-ounce) links	60 minutes	30 minutes	1 link

5 TB. kosher salt

2 TB. ground black pepper

1 TB. garlic powder

1 TB. ground caraway seeds

1 TB. ground coriander

2 tsp. mace

6 lb. lean elk, or substitute other game meat

4 lb. boneless pork shoulder with up to 1 lb. additional fat

2 TB. liquid smoke (optional)

1⅓ cup cold water

20 ft. hog casing or 32 mm collagen casing

1. In a small bowl, combine kosher salt, black pepper, garlic powder, caraway seeds, coriander, and mace. Set aside.

2. Cut elk and pork into cubes for grinding and place in a large bowl.

3. Using your hands or a wooden spoon, toss meat with spice mix until spices are evenly dispersed. Store in a covered container in the refrigerator or freezer until you're ready for the next step. Chill mixture for at least 30 minutes to improve grinding quality.

4. Grind mixture through a fine or medium plate (see Chapter 4).

5. Add liquid smoke (if using) and cold water to ground meat. Using your hands or a tabletop mixer, mix until the texture is consistent, about 5 minutes.

6. Make a test patty, cook it, taste it, and adjust seasonings as necessary.

7. Chill mixture in a covered container in the refrigerator or freezer until you're ready for the next step.

8. Stuff mixture in hog or collagen casing (see Chapter 4).

CHEF'S CHOICE

Elk and venison taste very similar, so you can replace the elk meat with venison if you prefer.

Bear Sausage

This is a very intense, gamey sausage, with notes of juniper that cut through the gamey taste and clear the palate. Don't reduce the amount of pork meat in this game sausage, as bear is the strongest tasting of all game meats.

Yield:	Prep time:	Cook time:	Serving size:
15 (5-ounce) links	60 minutes	30 minutes	1 link

2 TB. kosher salt

2 tsp. ground black pepper

1½ tsp. garlic powder

1 tsp. juniper berries, crushed

½ tsp. dried thyme leaves

3 lb. bear meat, trimmed of all fat

2 lb. boneless pork shoulder with up to ½ lb. additional fat

1 TB. liquid smoke (or to taste)

⅓ cup red wine vinegar

¼ cup water

10 ft. hog casing or 32 mm collagen casing

1. In a small bowl, combine kosher salt, black pepper, garlic powder, juniper berries, and thyme. Set aside.

2. Cut bear and pork into cubes for grinding and place in a large bowl.

3. Using your hands or a wooden spoon, toss meat with spice mix until spices are evenly dispersed. Store in a covered container in the refrigerator or freezer until you're ready for the next step. Chill mixture for at least 30 minutes to improve grinding quality.

4. Grind mixture through a fine or medium plate (see Chapter 4).

5. Add liquid smoke, red wine vinegar, and water to ground meat. Using your hands or a tabletop mixer, mix until the texture is consistent, about 5 minutes.

6. Make a test patty, cook it, taste it, and adjust seasonings as necessary.

7. Chill mixture in a covered container in the refrigerator or freezer until you're ready for the next step.

8. Stuff mixture in hog or collagen casing (see Chapter 4).

PRIME CUT

Bear meat tends to be a bit on the greasy side, with a rougher, coarse texture. According to some connoisseurs, the best bear meat comes from 2-year-old berry-eating bears.

Mediterranean Pheasant Sausage

This game sausage fuses Italian, Spanish, and Greek flavors to make a fresh-tasting sausage.

Yield:	Prep time:	Cook time:	Serving size:
12 (5-ounce) links	60 minutes	30 minutes	1 link

2 TB. kosher salt

3 TB. chopped fresh oregano

1½ TB. ground black pepper

2 TB. fresh garlic, finely chopped

2 tsp. fennel seed, crushed

2 tsp. fresh rosemary, finely chopped

Zest of one lemon, grated

3¼ lb. pheasant, or other game bird meat

¾ lb. pork fat

½ cup Madeira wine

8 ft. hog casing or 32 mm collagen casing

1. In a small bowl, combine kosher salt, oregano, black pepper, garlic, fennel seed, rosemary, and lemon zest. Set aside.

2. Cut pheasant and pork fat into cubes for grinding and place in a large bowl.

3. Using a wooden spoon or your hands, toss meat with spice mix until spices are evenly dispersed. Store in a covered container in the refrigerator or freezer until you're ready for the next step. Chill mixture for at least 30 minutes to improve grinding quality.

4. Grind mixture through a fine or medium plate (see Chapter 4).

5. Add Madeira wine to ground meat. Using your hands or a tabletop mixer, mix until the texture is consistent, about 5 minutes.

6. Make a test patty, cook it, taste it, and adjust seasonings as necessary.

7. Chill mixture in a covered container in the refrigerator or freezer until you're ready for the next step.

8. Stuff mixture in hog or collagen casing (see Chapter 4).

PRIME CUT

This is a good example of fusion cuisine, as it combines different spice traditions from around the Mediterranean with an American game bird.

Rabbit Sausage

This mild game sausage has a medley of French herbs and a little kick of cayenne.

Yield:	Prep time:	Cook time:	Serving size:
12 (5-ounce) links	60 minutes	30 minutes	1 link

2 TB. kosher salt

1 TB. fresh garlic, finely chopped

2 tsp. ground white pepper

1 tsp. ground black pepper

1 tsp. yellow mustard seed, crushed

1 tsp. dried sage

1 tsp. dried rosemary

1 tsp. dried thyme

1 tsp. sugar

½ tsp. cayenne pepper

3½ lb. wild rabbit meat, or substitute domestically raised

½ lb. bacon

1 TB. white wine vinegar

1¼ cup heavy cream

4 egg whites

8 ft. hog casing or 32 mm collagen casing

1. In a small bowl, combine kosher salt, garlic, white pepper, black pepper, yellow mustard seed, sage, rosemary, thyme, sugar, and cayenne pepper. Set aside.

2. Cut rabbit and bacon into cubes for grinding and place in a large mixing bowl.

3. Using your hands or a wooden spoon, toss meat with spice mix until spices are evenly dispersed. Store in a covered container in the refrigerator or freezer until you're ready for the next step. Chill mixture for at least 30 minutes to improve grinding quality.

4. Grind mixture through a fine or medium plate (see Chapter 4).

5. Add white wine vinegar, heavy cream, and egg whites to ground meat. Using your hands or a tabletop mixer, mix until the texture is consistent, about 5 minutes.

6. Make a test patty, cook it, taste it, and adjust seasonings as necessary.

7. Chill mixture in a covered container in the refrigerator or freezer until you're ready for the next step.

8. Stuff mixture in hog or collagen casing (see Chapter 4).

PRIME CUT

Rabbit is one of the mildest game meats and, if possible, you should use wild rabbit in this recipe. Farm-raised rabbit meat is known for tasting like chicken.

Cooking with Sausage

Wow! We've covered a lot of recipes, and by now, you can make a brat with the best of them. But we're not quite finished yet. These next four chapters complete your artisan sausage making experience. In them, we introduce you to the art of curing and smoking sausages, cover condiment and accompaniment recipes, and offer recipes for using your artisan sausages. We also detail cooking techniques for sausages, explain how to set up a sausage platter, offer pairing suggestions for your sausages, and suggest entertaining tips for using sausages.

Curing and Smoking Your Sausages

In This Chapter

- Safety procedures for curing and smoking sausages
- Smoking equipment and curing powders
- How to cure sausages
- How to smoke sausages
- Recipes for cured and smoked sausages

Curing and smoking sausages is a little more involved than making fresh bulk and linked sausages. Though it's not difficult to cure or to smoke sausages, you should already be familiar with the overall sausage making process before you move on to making beef jerky or smoked brats.

Smoking and curing add a delicious intensity to meats and spices. Smoking, in particular, adds a real depth and complexity to meat. Grilled burgers, for example, taste better than fried patties. It's the same with sausages—the flavor of smoke just enhances the meat.

Some sausages, including knackwurst and andouille, are known to be smoked and cured. Game sausages also are often smoked and cured. This chapter includes some delicious recipes for knackwurst, andouille, and game sausages, as well as cured Chinese sausages and even beef jerky and snack sticks. Trust us: once you make your own jerky, you'll never buy a Slim Jim again!

Safely Curing and Smoking Meat

Curing and smoking adds another step to the sausage making process. That means you are handling raw meat for a longer period of time and, because of that, you should be extra vigilant about following the safety recommendations in Chapter 3.

Raw meat, poultry, and seafood should only be kept at room temperature, i.e., on the counter, for a *total of 4 hours* (and, ideally, only 2 or 3 hours) before cooking. Because you don't want to use up those 4 hours before you get to the curing or smoking stage, you should be comfortable processing the meat—the cubing, the grinding, and the linking—so that it takes less time. You want to be adept and confident at fresh sausage making before you try your hand at curing or smoking.

When you cook fresh sausages correctly, you kill any bacteria that are present. When you cure or air-dry sausages without smoking or cooking, you aren't cooking them. Instead, you are removing the moisture, which prevents many germs that cause food poisoning from growing, as many microbes can't grow in dry environments.

Don't Botch It: Watch Out for Botulism

One particularly nasty—and sometimes deadly—microorganism thrives in an *anaerobic* environment: *Clostridium botulinum*, or botulism. Botulism thrives in temperatures between 40°F and 140°F, and it loves anaerobic conditions. Unfortunately, this is just the kind of condition that occurs when you smoke or dry sausages.

To keep this harmful bacteria out of your sausages, add *nitrites* and *nitrates*. In particular, you need sodium nitrite and sodium nitrate. Nitrites and nitrates are chemicals that prevent botulism and other bacteria from growing and spreading, and they also prevent fats in meats from going rancid. Nitrites also give cured meats their distinctive pink color and cured taste.

 DEFINITION

Anaerobic means without oxygen. An anaerobic environment is one in which there is no oxygen present.

Nitrites and **nitrates** are naturally occurring chemicals that have nitrogen in them, which prevent botulism. For curing and smoking, the chemicals you need are sodium nitrite and sodium nitrate.

Using nitrites and nitrates in foods isn't without controversy, however. When some nitrites and nitrates break down in your body, they form cancer-causing compounds. Some studies have shown that eating too many cured meats with nitrites and nitrates can increase the risk of cancer. Other, conflicting studies say that people consume more naturally occurring nitrates in vegetables.

The USDA and FDA have strict guidelines on how much sodium nitrate and sodium nitrite to use in sausage and cured meats. However, they *never, ever* recommend making sausage or cured meats without nitrites. There is no acceptable substitute for sodium nitrate and sodium nitrite when making cured sausages, and the benefits—not dying from botulism—outweigh the potential cancer risks.

> **PRIME CUT**
>
> Sausage makers traditionally used saltpeter or potassium nitrite to kill botulism. The USDA advises again using potassium nitrite because it contains a very high concentration of nitrite, which can cause other health concerns.

If you have concerns about using nitrates or nitrites, you're better off making fresh sausages.

A Recipe for a Cure: Curing Powders

You can get sodium nitrite and sodium nitrate in *curing powders* or *curing salts*.

> **DEFINITION**
>
> **Curing powders,** also sometimes called **curing salts,** are commercial mixes of table salt (sodium chloride), sodium nitrite, and/or sodium nitrate. You must use them when making cured and smoked sausages.

These commercial mixes contain table salt, sodium nitrite, and/or sodium nitrate. Some contain just sodium nitrite, and others contain a blend with sodium nitrate. If you're smoking sausages, use one that just contains sodium nitrite; if you're curing, you also need sodium nitrate, as it takes longer to break down than sodium nitrite.

Some of the name brands of curing powders include Insta Cure, Prague Powder, and DQ Curing Powder. Each brand has two different cure mixes, called #1 or #2. No matter what the brand, the different numbers indicate the following ingredients:

- **Curing powder #1:** Contains 6.25 percent sodium nitrite, with the remainder table salt, plus a little red food coloring to alert the user that it's not table salt.

- **Curing powder #2:** Contains 6.25 percent sodium nitrite and 4 percent sodium nitrate, with the remainder table salt, plus the same red food coloring as #1. Cure powder #2 is typically used for recipes that take more time.

On average, recipes call for about 1 teaspoon per 5 pounds of meat. The recipes in this chapter tell you whether you need curing powder #1 or #2.

You might have heard about some "natural cures" for curing sausages. These natural cures—sometimes made of celery and other vegetables with naturally occurring nitrates—are supposed to be able to take the place of curing powders. We don't recommend them. The actual quantities of nitrates in them can vary, and you could easily underdose or overdose your sausage with them.

THE GRIND

Don't use "natural cures" for curing your sausages. You can't guarantee you are getting the amount of nitrates and nitrites you need to kill harmful microbes. Instead, use a brand-name curing powder with exact amounts of nitrates and nitrites.

You might see Morton's Tender Quick on the shelves when you're shopping for curing powder. It contains sodium nitrite and sodium nitrate, along with salt, sugar, and other chemicals like propylene glycol (which is actually used to de-ice airplanes). It isn't interchangeable with cure powder #1 or #2. This cure is typically used for brines rather than sausage making.

Curing Sausages

When you cure sausages, you basically air-dry them. To prevent the meat from going bad, you need to add the curing powder either before or after you grind your sausages but before you link them. Make sure that the curing powder is thoroughly mixed into the meat.

After you link your sausages, hang them out to dry or cure. If you live in a very cold climate, you can hang them in a clean, cool, dry place for several days until the sausages are dry and moisture free.

If you don't live in such a climate or don't really want to have sausages hanging in your garage for several days or weeks, you can use the quick cure method.

The Quick Cure Method

Rather than leaving your sausages hanging in your garage for days on end, we recommend using the quick cure method for all cured recipes in this chapter. Not only is it easier, it's safer if you live anywhere that temperatures vary considerably.

After linking your sausages, hang them up in a refrigerator that has nothing else in it. If you want to keep other items in the fridge, you can put the sausages in an airtight container and then put them in your fridge for 2 to 3 days.

After the sausages have cured in the refrigerator for a few days, heat up your oven to the lowest setting possible—about 170°F to 180°F. Let the sausages dry in your oven for 3 to 8 hours, as suggested by each recipe. This process dries out your sausage without cooking it.

Smoking Sausages

You can smoke your sausages using the hot smoking method or the cold smoking method. As you might have guessed, the main difference between the two techniques is temperature. If you smoke the sausages or meats at less than 165°F, it's considered cold smoking. Anything above 165°F is considered hot smoking. More precisely, cold smoking is generally done between 90°F and 120°F, and hot smoking is generally done between 170°F and 300°F.

Typically, cold smoking involves smoking meats for 8 to 12 hours, but some recipes call for smoking the meat for up to 3 days. For hot smoking, you generally only smoke the meat for 1 to 3 hours, depending on the recipe.

You must use curing salts if you are cold smoking your sausages because the sausages will not reach high-enough temperatures to kill any germs present in the meat.

Not everyone agrees that hot smoking requires curing salts. That's because when you hot smoke sausages and ensure that they reach an internal temperature of 165°F, you are cooking them. Basically, it's a form of roasting or baking, but with smoke. This is the technique used for smoked brats and kielbasas.

Some experts say that hot smoking still poses a risk for botulism. For this reason, many people prefer to add curing powders just to stay on the safe side if they're not planning to further cook the meat. If you plan to cook the sausage—fry, poach, or grill it—before eating it, you don't need to use curing powder, as the cooking process will kill any microbes.

THE GRIND

Whether or not you use curing powder in your hot smoked sausages, it's important to keep in mind that they're as perishable as any type of roasted or baked meats. They should be eaten or frozen within a few days.

Kinds of Smokers

In order to smoke sausages, you need a smoker. Generally, smokers cost about $100 and fall into the following three categories:

- **Barbecue smokers:** These are basically tricked out barbecue grills. They're not the best choice for smoking sausages, as they're primarily intended for barbecuing meats. You can smoke sausages in these smokers, but doing so requires a fair bit of tinkering and tending to ensure the sausages are smoked at the required temperatures.

- **Kettle or water smokers:** These kettlelike contraptions have one or more racks for the sausages and a fire pan for wood or charcoal. They usually have a water pan as well.

- **Cabinet smokers:** These look like mini-refrigerators and contain racks, a box for wood or charcoal, and a heating element (usually electric). The cabinet smoker is the most versatile of all the smokers, but if you're just starting to smoke, you may not want to invest in one until you're sure you enjoy making smoked sausages.

You can also make your own smoker (there are plenty of instructions available on the Internet), using two 55-gallon metal garbage cans.

You need a digital, oven-safe thermometer to double-check your smoker's temperature gauge. Although smokers come with their own temperature gauge—some smokers don't even have an exact temperature gauge.

How to Smoke Sausage

You typically smoke sausages after stuffing and linking them, but you can also leave the sausage as one giant link to be cut after smoking. The smoking process is relatively simple, but follow a few guidelines to help make the process smooth.

First, make sure your sausages are dry before you smoke them. This ensures a more even smoking process and produces a uniform, brown color. You can dry your sausages in either of the following ways:

- Air-dry them in a cool environment, perhaps an empty refrigerator, for a day or two.

- Dry them in the smoker. To dry the sausages in the smoker, heat your smoker to between 90°F and 100°F, open all the dampers so the moisture can escape, and put your sausages in the smoker. Leave the sausages in the smoker at the same temperature until they are dry to the touch; it will take a couple hours.

PRIME CUT

Different woods create different flavor profiles for your sausage. Hardwood such as hickory, oak, apple, cherry, and mesquite are all good choices. You can also use hardwood briquettes and even chips from old oak wine barrels.

Be sure to follow the instructions that come with your smoker. In addition, keep the following tips in mind:

Don't use gasoline, lighter fluid, or any other kind of accelerant to start the fire in your smoker. These fluids create fumes, which can contaminate your sausages. Many smokers have electric starters, which require only the push of a button.

Use the type and size of wood recommended for your smoker. Some smokers suggest that you soak hard wood chips in water before smoking; others do not. Some recommend using wood chunks, which are larger than wood chips. They smoke for a longer period of time than chips and you don't have to replace them in your smoker as frequently. Many smokers also recommend that you use some damp sawdust because that produces a fire with less heat that's easy to control. Follow the directions for your smoker in this instance.

THE GRIND

It's best not to use softwoods such as cedar or pine because the smoke these woods create are sooty and oily and impart off tastes to your sausages.

Frequently check the temperature while smoking. The air should stay between 225°F and 300°F during the hot smoking process. For cold smoking, it should stay between 90°F and 120°F. A good, oven-safe digital thermometer should do the job quite nicely.

Tend to your smoker frequently to ensure that the wood doesn't burn out before your sausage is completely smoked. In general, it takes between 1 and 3 hours for a hot smoke. A sausage stuffed in hog casings takes about 2 hours, provided the heat is around 225°F and you don't open the chamber frequently, which would cool it down.

How do you know your meat is completely smoked? When it looks like it is completely smoked, take a digital meat thermometer and insert it into the center of the sausage. If the temperature is at least 165°, it's done.

After you smoke your sausages, rinse them in cool water to stop the cooking process. Pat them dry with paper towels and serve them immediately or refrigerate them. You can then either serve them cold or reheated, or you can package them and freeze for later use.

Smoked Venison Sausage

This is a mild game sausage, with a distinct tang of juniper berries.

Yield:	Prep time:	Cook time:	Serving size:
15 (5-ounce) links	60 minutes	30 minutes	1 link

1½ TB. kosher salt

1 tsp. cure powder #1

1 TB. sugar

1 TB. onion powder

2 tsp. ground black pepper

2 tsp. juniper berries, crushed

1 tsp. garlic powder

1 tsp. dried sage

3 lb. lean venison meat

1 lb. boneless pork shoulder

1 lb. pork fat

¾ cup ice water

10 ft. hog casing or 32 mm collagen casing

1. In a small bowl, combine kosher salt, cure powder #1, sugar, onion powder, black pepper, juniper berries, garlic powder, and sage. Set aside.

2. Cut venison, pork, and pork fat into cubes for grinding and place in a large mixing bowl.

3. Using your hands or a wooden spoon, toss meat with spice mix until spices are evenly dispersed. Store in a covered container in the refrigerator or freezer until you're ready for the next step. Chill mixture for at least 30 minutes to improve grinding quality.

4. Grind mixture through a fine or medium plate (see Chapter 4).

5. Add ice water to ground meat. Using your hands or a tabletop mixer, mix until the texture is consistent, about 5 minutes.

6. Make a test patty, cook it, taste it, and adjust seasoning as necessary.

7. Chill mixture in a covered container in the refrigerator or freezer until you're ready for the next step.

8. Stuff mixture in hog or collagen casing (see Chapter 4).

9. Cure for 24 hours.

10. Hot smoke following your smoker's instructions.

Venison or Beef Snack Sticks

Forget those snack sticks you buy at a gas station or convenience store. These savory, smoked sausage sticks pop with flavors of garlic, onion, and just a touch of cayenne.

Yield:	Prep time:	Cook time:	Serving size:
12 (5-ounce) links	60 minutes	30 minutes	1 link

2 TB. kosher salt	1 tsp. cayenne
1 tsp. cure powder #1	4½ lb. lean venison or beef
2 tsp. ground black pepper	½ lb. beef or pork fat
1 tsp. mustard powder	½ cup ice water
2 tsp. onion powder	20 ft. sheep casing or 24 mm collagen casing
1 tsp. celery seed	
2 tsp. garlic powder	

1. In a small bowl, combine kosher salt, cure powder #1, black pepper, mustard powder, onion powder, celery seed, garlic powder, and cayenne. Set aside.

2. Cut venison and fat into cubes for grinding and place in a large mixing bowl.

3. Using your hands or a wooden spoon, toss meat with spice mix until spices are evenly dispersed. Store in a covered container in the refrigerator or freezer until you're ready for the next step. Chill mixture for at least 30 minutes to improve grinding quality.

4. Grind mixture through a fine plate (see Chapter 4).

5. Add ice water to ground meat. Using your hands or a tabletop mixer, mix until the texture is consistent, about 5 minutes.

6. Make a test patty, cook it, taste it, and adjust seasoning as necessary.

7. Chill mixture in a covered container in the refrigerator or freezer until you're ready for the next step.

8. Stuff mixture in sheep or collagen casing (see Chapter 4).

9. Cure sausages overnight in the refrigerator.

10. Preheat oven to lowest possible temperature setting (170°F is ideal) and place sticks on the lowest oven rack. Leave the oven open a crack to allow the moisture from the sausages to escape. Cook sausages for 3 to 4 hours or until their internal temperature reaches 155°F.

Variation: You can cold smoke these snack sticks following your smoker's instructions after curing them overnight.

CHEF'S CHOICE

Feel free to use other game meats (same quantity), such as elk and rabbit, in these snack sticks.

Beef or Venison Jerky

This chewy, smoky jerky stick boasts savory flavors of onion and garlic. A lot of jerky recipes don't require grinding; instead, they're just strips of cured meat. Because this recipe requires grinding, this jerky has a more tender texture.

Yield:	Prep time:	Cook time:	Serving size:
30 ounces dry jerky	60 minutes	30 minutes	1 link

1½ TB. kosher salt

1 tsp. cure powder #1

2 TB. ground black pepper

1 tsp. garlic powder

2 tsp. onion powder

4½ lb. lean beef (90 percent meat) or venison

½ lb. beef or pork fat

1½ TB. Worcestershire sauce

1 TB. soy sauce

1 TB. liquid smoke

1. In a small bowl, combine kosher salt, cure powder #1, black pepper, garlic powder, and onion powder. Set aside.

2. Cut beef and beef fat into cubes for grinding and place in a large mixing bowl.

3. Using your hands or a wooden spoon, toss meat with spice mix until spices are evenly dispersed. Store in a covered container in the refrigerator or freezer until you're ready for the next step. Chill mixture for at least 30 minutes to improve grinding quality.

4. Grind mixture through a medium plate (see Chapter 4).

5. Add Worcestershire sauce, soy sauce, and liquid smoke to ground meat. Using your hands or a tabletop mixer, mix until the texture is consistent, about 5 minutes.

6. Make a test patty, cook it, taste it, and adjust seasonings as necessary.

7. Chill mixture in a covered container in the refrigerator or freezer until you're ready for the next step.

8. Use a *jerky gun* to pipe strips of meat onto cookie racks and proceed to step 9.

If you don't have a jerky gun, line a 9×9-inch baking pan with two 2-foot lengths of plastic wrap. Pack meat mixture into pan to form a solid loaf with no air packets. Fold the plastic wrap over meat to seal it. Put loaf in the freezer for 2 hours or until meat is very firm. Remove meat from pan and peel off plastic wrap. Thinly slice meat and lay onto racks and proceed to step 9.

9. Preheat the oven to the lowest possible temperature (170°F is ideal). Leave oven door cracked open to allow the moisture to escape. Leave jerky in heated oven for 6 to 8 hours or until fully dehydrated. (Alternatively use a food dehydrator, following manufacturer's instructions.)

Variation: You can change the flavor profile of this jerky by replacing the combined amounts of Worcestershire sauce, liquid smoke, and soy sauce with a prepared barbecue sauce, buffalo sauce, or teriyaki sauce.

DEFINITION

A **jerky gun** is a piping tool for making beef jerky. It looks similar to a cookie dough shooter or a pastry gun, but it is used for meat.

Sichuan-Style Cured Lop Cheong

This cured Asian sausage is sweet and spicy. It tastes great in eggrolls, stir-fries, and even on a bun with your favorite condiments.

Yield:	Prep time:	Cook time:	Serving size:
15 (5-ounce) links	60 minutes	30 minutes	1 link

1½ TB. kosher salt

1 tsp. cure powder #2

1 TB. sugar

1 tsp. ground white pepper

2 TB. chili powder

1 tsp. Chinese five-spice powder

1 tsp. ground Sichuan peppercorns

5 lb. boneless pork shoulder with up to ½ lb. additional fat

¼ cup soy sauce

3 TB. white liquor, such as vodka or *sake*

12 ft. hog casing or 32 mm collagen casing

1. In a small bowl, combine kosher salt, cure powder #2, sugar, white pepper, chili powder, Chinese five-spice powder, and Sichuan peppercorns. Set aside.

2. Cut pork into cubes for grinding and place in a large mixing bowl.

3. Using your hands or a wooden spoon, toss pork with spice mix until spices are evenly dispersed. Store in a covered container in the refrigerator or freezer until you're ready for the next step. Chill mixture for at least 30 minutes to improve grinding quality.

4. Grind mixture through a fine or medium plate (see Chapter 4).

5. Add soy sauce and white liquor to ground meat. Using your hands or a tabletop mixer, mix until the texture is consistent, about 5 minutes.

6. Make a test patty, cook it, taste it, and adjust seasonings as necessary.

7. Chill mixture in a covered container in the refrigerator or freezer until you're ready for the next step.

8. Stuff mixture in hog or collagen casing (see Chapter 4) and hang to cure for 3 days.

9. Steam sausages for 20 to 30 minutes or until internal temperature reaches 165°F.

10. Use fresh or cool sausages and store in the refrigerator or freezer for later use.

DEFINITION

Sake (pronounced *SOCK-eh*) is a rice-based alcoholic beverage. Although sometimes referred to as a "rice wine," its fermenting process is actually more similar to that of beer than wine. It typically has about 18 to 20 percent alcohol.

Smoked Polish Sausage

If you love garlic, you'll love this garlicky, smoky link.

Yield:	Prep time:	Cook time:	Serving size:
15 (5-ounce) links	60 minutes	30 minutes	1 link

1½ TB. kosher salt

1 tsp. cure powder #1

8 cloves fresh garlic, finely chopped

2 TB. sweet Hungarian paprika

2 tsp. finely ground black pepper

2 tsp. dried marjoram

5 lb. boneless pork shoulder with up to ½ lb. additional fat

¾ cup water

10 ft. hog casing or 32 mm collagen casing

1. In a small bowl, combine kosher salt, cure powder #1, garlic, sweet Hungarian paprika, black pepper, and marjoram. Set aside.

2. Cut pork into cubes for grinding and place in a large mixing bowl.

3. Using your hands or a wooden spoon, toss meat with spice mix until spices are evenly dispersed. Store in a covered container in the refrigerator or freezer until you're ready for the next step. Chill mixture for at least 30 minutes to improve grinding quality.

4. Grind mixture through a fine or medium plate (see Chapter 4).

5. Add water to ground meat. Using your hands or a tabletop mixer, mix until the texture is consistent, about 5 minutes.

6. Make a test patty, cook it, taste it, and adjust seasoning as necessary.

7. Chill mixture in a covered container in the refrigerator or freezer until you're ready for the next step.

8. Stuff mixture in hog or collagen casing (see Chapter 4).

9. Cure for 24 hours and then hot smoke following your smoker's instructions.

PRIME CUT

Smoked Polish sausage, or *polska kielbasa wedzona* in Polish, is believed to be the most popular type of Polish sausage in the world. The first Polish immigrants likely brought this recipe with them to the United States.

Smoked Pheasant Sausage

This meaty game sausage sings with sage and smoke.

Yield:	Prep time:	Cook time:	Serving size:
12 (5-ounce) links	60 minutes	30 minutes	1 link

1½ TB. kosher salt

1 tsp. cure powder #1

2 TB. sugar

2 TB. ground white pepper

3 TB. poultry seasoning

1 TB. onion powder

4 lb. pheasant meat, any cuts

1 lb. *fatback pork*

¾ cup water

10 ft. hog casing or 32 mm collagen casing

1. In a small bowl, combine kosher salt, cure powder #1, sugar, white pepper, poultry seasoning, and onion powder. Set aside.

2. Cut pheasant and fatback pork into cubes for grinding and place in a large mixing bowl.

3. Using your hands or a wooden spoon, toss meat with spice mix until spices are evenly dispersed. Store in a covered container in the refrigerator or freezer until you're ready for the next step. Chill mixture for at least 30 minutes to improve grinding quality.

4. Grind mixture through a fine or medium plate (see Chapter 4).

5. Add water to ground meat. Using your hands or a tabletop mixer, mix until the texture is consistent, about 5 minutes.

6. Make a test patty, cook it, taste it, and adjust seasoning as necessary.

7. Chill mixture in a covered container in the refrigerator or freezer until you're ready for the next step.

8. Stuff mixture in hog or collagen casing (see Chapter 4).

9. Cure for 24 hours, and then hot smoke following your smoker's instructions.

DEFINITION

Fatback pork is a cut of pork taken off the hog's back, and it is virtually all fat. It is similar to the white portion of bacon.

Spicy Lamb Sausage

Hot and sweet, this lamb sausage tastes a little bit like mild gyro meat.

Yield:	Prep time:	Cook time:	Serving size:
12 (5-ounce) links	60 minutes	30 minutes	1 link

1 TB. kosher salt

1 tsp. cure powder #1

3 TB. garlic, chopped

2 TB. shallots, chopped

½ tsp. ground black pepper

½ tsp. red pepper flakes

1 tsp. Spanish hot paprika

1 tsp. ground coriander

1 TB. honey

½ TB. dried thyme

½ tsp. dried parsley

½ tsp. dried rosemary

3 lb. boneless lamb shoulder

½ lb. pork fat

½ lb. *pancetta*

¾ cup chicken stock or water

8 ft. hog casing or 32 mm collagen casing

1. In a small bowl, combine kosher salt, cure powder #1, garlic, shallots, black pepper, red pepper, Spanish hot paprika, coriander, honey, thyme, parsley, and rosemary.

2. Cut lamb, pork fat, and pancetta into cubes for grinding and place in a large mixing bowl.

3. Using your hands or a wooden spoon, toss meat with spice mix until spices are evenly dispersed. Store in a covered container in the refrigerator or freezer until you're ready for the next step. Chill mixture for at least 30 minutes to improve grinding quality.

4. Grind mixture through a fine or medium plate (see Chapter 4).

5. Add chicken stock to ground meat. Using your hands or a tabletop mixer, mix until the texture is consistent, about 5 minutes.

6. Make a test patty, cook it, taste it, and adjust seasonings as necessary.

7. Chill mixture in a covered container in the refrigerator or freezer until you're ready for the next step.

8. Stuff mixture in hog or collagen casing (see Chapter 4).

9. Cure for 24 hours, and then hot smoke following smoker's instructions.

Variation: For a phenomenal fresh sausage, eliminate the cure powder and increase the kosher salt to 2 tablespoons.

DEFINITION

Pancetta is a type of Italian bacon that's typically cured with spices such as peppercorns, fennel, and nutmeg.

Knackwurst Sausage

This short and plump smoked sausage tastes of garlic and sweet Hungarian paprika.

Yield:	Prep time:	Cook time:	Serving size:
12 (5-ounce) links	60 minutes	30 minutes	1 link

1½ TB. kosher salt

1 tsp. cure powder #1

2 TB. ground black pepper

1 TB. ground white pepper

1 TB. sweet Hungarian paprika

6 cloves garlic, finely chopped

2 tsp. ground mace

½ tsp. ground nutmeg

½ tsp. ground coriander

½ tsp. ground allspice

2½ lb. boneless beef shoulder

2½ lb. boneless pork shoulder with up to ½ lb. additional fat

½ cup ice water

10 ft. hog casing or 32 mm collagen casing

1. In a small bowl, combine kosher salt, cure powder #1, black pepper, white pepper, sweet Hungarian paprika, garlic, mace, nutmeg, coriander, and allspice. Set aside.

2. Cut beef and pork into cubes for grinding and place in a large mixing bowl.

3. Using your hands or a wooden spoon, toss meat with spice mix until spices are evenly dispersed. Store in a covered container in the refrigerator or freezer until you're ready for the next step. Chill mixture for at least 30 minutes to improve grinding quality.

4. Grind mixture through a fine or medium plate (see Chapter 4).

5. Add ice water to ground meat. Using your hands or a tabletop mixer, mix until the texture is consistent, about 5 minutes.

6. Make a test patty, cook it, test it, and adjust seasonings as necessary.

7. Chill mixture in a covered container in the refrigerator or freezer until you're ready for the next step.

8. Stuff mixture in hog or collagen casing (see Chapter 4).

9. Cure for 24 hours, and then hot smoke following smoker's instructions.

Variation: To make a fresh, unsmoked version of this sausage, add 2 tablespoons liquid smoke, leave out the curing powder, and increase the amount of salt to $2\frac{1}{2}$ tablespoons.

PRIME CUT

Knackwurst is one of the few German sausages that contain garlic. Originating in the Holstein area of Germany, Knackwursts are typically served with sauerkraut or sweet and sour cabbage.

Andouille Sausage

This spicy hot Louisiana sausage is rich in garlic with hints of thyme and paprika dancing in the background.

Yield:	Prep time:	Cook time:	Serving size:
12 (5-ounce) links	60 minutes	30 minutes	1 link

1½ TB. kosher salt

1 tsp. cure powder #1

4 TB. chopped fresh garlic

2 TB. ground black pepper

4 tsp. Spanish hot paprika

1 TB. fresh thyme leaves, minced

1 tsp. cayenne

1 tsp. red pepper flakes

5 lb. boneless pork shoulder with up to ½ lb. additional fat

¾ cup water

10 ft. hog casing or 32 mm collagen casing

1. In a small bowl, combine kosher salt, cure powder #1, garlic, black pepper, Spanish hot paprika, thyme, cayenne, and red pepper flakes. Set aside.

2. Cut pork into cubes for grinding and place in a large mixing bowl.

3. Using your hands or a wooden spoon, toss meat with spice mix until spices are evenly dispersed. Store in a covered container in the refrigerator or freezer until you're ready for the next step. Chill mixture for at least 30 minutes to improve grinding quality.

4. Grind mixture through a fine or medium plate (see Chapter 4).

5. Add water to ground meat. Using your hands or a tabletop mixer, mix until the texture is consistent, about 5 minutes.

6. Make a test patty, cook it, taste it, and adjust seasonings as necessary.

7. Chill mixture in a covered container in the refrigerator or freezer until you're ready for the next step.

8. Stuff mixture in hog or collagen casing (see Chapter 4).

9. Cure for 24 hours, and then hot smoke following smoker's instructions.

PRIME CUT

If you're ever in LaPlace, Louisiana, the third weekend of October, head to the annual Andouille Festival. There's a gumbo cook-off, a pageant and, of course, lots of sausage.

Sausage Condiments and Accompaniments

In This Chapter

- Condiment recipes
- Accompaniment recipes

If you're going to go to all the trouble of making your own frankfurter or seafood sausage, you might as well spend a little extra time and make your own condiments and other tasty sausage accompaniments.

Every sausage in this book tastes great on its own, but adding a dash of homemade mustard, catsup, or horseradish sauce just might make the difference between a tasty repast and the best link you've ever sunk your teeth into. And slathering that sausage with homemade caramelized onions will send even the most cynical sausage connoisseur into hog heaven.

Although making your own sauces might sound daunting, it's nothing compared to the steps involved in linking sausages. So instead of buying fine mustard, gourmet ketchup, or specialty barbecue sauce to accompany your homemade links, take a little extra time to prepare these condiments yourself. Doing so pays off in major taste bud dividends.

The recipes for condiments and other sausage accessories included in this chapter are great to make for parties, picnics, and grill-outs. And many of these accentuate other foods besides sausages.

German Mustard

Slightly spicy and acidic, this mustard is made to accompany German sausages.

Yield:	Cook time:	Marinate time:	Serving size:
1½–2 cups	30 minutes	3 days	1 tablespoon

¼ cup yellow mustard seed

2 TB. black or brown mustard seed, heaping

¼ cup dry mustard powder

½ cup water

1½ cups apple cider vinegar

1 small onion, chopped

2 TB. firmly packed brown sugar

1 tsp. salt

2 garlic gloves, chopped

½ tsp. ground cinnamon

¼ tsp. ground allspice

¼ tsp. tarragon leaves, crushed

¼ tsp. ground dill seeds

⅛ tsp. ground turmeric

1. In a small bowl, combine yellow mustard seed, black mustard seed, and dry mustard powder.

2. In a 1-quart saucepan, combine water, apple cider vinegar, onion, brown sugar, salt, garlic, cinnamon, allspice, tarragon, dill, and turmeric. Bring to a boil over high heat and reduce heat to medium. Cook uncovered until reduced by half, about 10 to 15 minutes.

3. Pour hot mixture over mustard mixture. Let mixture stand at room temperature, covered, overnight, preferably for 24 hours. If necessary, add more vinegar to maintain enough liquid to cover seeds.

4. Process in a blender for 3 to 4 minutes, or until desired consistency is achieved.

5. Store mustard in a covered container or jars in the refrigerator.

6. Age for at least 2 more days before serving. Mustard will last for up to a year in the refrigerator.

CHEF'S CHOICE

To make horseradish mustard, mix 1 tablespoon mustard with 1 teaspoon prepared horseradish. Serve immediately or store in the refrigerator for up to a week.

Easy Dijon Mustard

This Dijon mustard tastes slightly sweet and so good that you're going to "pass" on the poupon.

Yield:	Cook time:	Marinate time:	Serving size:
1½–2 cups	30 minutes	2 days	1 tablespoon

2 cloves garlic, finely chopped

1 cup yellow onion, chopped

2 cups dry white wine

1 cup dry mustard

1 TB. vegetable oil

2 TB. honey

2 tsp. kosher salt

4 drops hot pepper sauce or to taste

1. Add garlic, yellow onion, and dry white wine to a small saucepan and bring to a boil over medium-high heat. Reduce heat to medium-low and simmer for 5 minutes, then remove from heat to cool for 5 minutes.

2. Strain cooled mixture into a medium saucepan to remove solids.

3. Add dry mustard to strained wine and mix with a whisk until the texture is smooth. Add vegetable oil, honey, kosher salt, and hot pepper sauce and mix with whisk.

4. Put the pan on medium-low heat and stir constantly with whisk for 3 to 4 minutes, until the mixture thickens slightly. (It will continue to thicken as it cools.)

5. Remove mustard from heat, let it cool, and store, in a covered container or portioned into jars, in the refrigerator.

6. Age for at least 2 days before serving. Mustard will last for up to 4 months in the refrigerator.

CHEF'S CHOICE

While this mustard tastes amazing on sausages, you can also use it in salad dressings, serve it on burgers, or use it as a dipping sauce for pretzels.

Chinese Hot Mustard

Chinese mustard is the simplest mustard to make, as it only requires dry mustard and hot water. Adding optional sugar and oil balances out the potent heat.

Yield:	Cook time:	Marinate time:	Serving size:
about ⅓ cup	10 minutes	2–4 hours	1 teaspoon

¼ cup dry mustard

½ tsp. sugar (optional)

¼ cup boiling water

2 tsp. vegetable oil (optional)

1. In a small bowl, combine dry mustard and sugar (if using).

2. Pour boiling water over mustard and mix with a metal spoon.

3. Mix in vegetable oil (if using) until combined.

4. Let mustard stand, covered, for 2 to 4 hours.

5. Serve immediately or store, in a covered container or portioned into jars, in the refrigerator. The mustard will diminish in flavor quickly and is best used within a day or two.

PRIME CUT

You can control how hot this mustard becomes in two ways. The longer you mix it in step 2, the hotter it will become; and the longer you let it steep—for up to 4 hours—the hotter it gets.

Mayonnaise

Creamy and smooth, there's nothing that tastes quite as good as homemade mayonnaise.

Yield:	Prep time:	Serving size:
1 quart	30 minutes	1 tablespoon

3 egg yolks, from pasteurized eggs

2 TB. white vinegar

2 TB. water

2 tsp. dry mustard powder

1 tsp. sea salt or to taste

1 tsp. white pepper or to taste

2 TB. lemon juice or to taste

3 cups vegetable oil

2 dashes hot pepper sauce or to taste

1. In a food processor, combine egg yolks, white vinegar, water, dry mustard powder, $\frac{1}{2}$ teaspoon sea salt, $\frac{1}{2}$ teaspoon white pepper, and 1 tablespoon lemon juice. Pulse until slightly foamy.

2. Add vegetable oil at a slow, constant pour while running the processor. This will take up to a couple minutes to finish. If oil starts to pool on the surface of mixture, slow the pace of your pour.

3. Season to taste with remaining $\frac{1}{2}$ teaspoon sea salt, remaining $\frac{1}{2}$ teaspoon white pepper, remaining 1 tablespoon lemon juice, and hot pepper sauce.

4. Chill immediately in a covered container. Mayonnaise will keep for several days in the refrigerator.

THE GRIND

Because the eggs are uncooked in this recipe, you should use pasteurized eggs. Pasteurized eggs have been heated to a specific temperature for a controlled period of time, which destroys any salmonella or other microorganisms that may be in the eggs.

Aioli

Aioli is simply a garlicky good mayonnaise.

Yield:	Prep time:	Serving size:
1 quart	30 minutes	1 tablespoon

3 egg yolks, from pasteurized eggs

1 TB. red wine vinegar

1 TB. garlic paste

1 tsp. sea salt or to taste

2 tsp. lemon juice or to taste

1 cup olive oil

2 cups vegetable oil

1. In a food processor, combine egg yolks, red wine vinegar, garlic paste, $\frac{1}{2}$ teaspoon sea salt, and 1 teaspoon lemon juice. Pulse until slightly foamy.

2. Add olive oil and vegetable oil at a slow, constant pour while running the processor. This will take up to a couple minutes to finish. If oil starts to pool on the surface, slow the pace of your pour.

3. Season to taste with remaining $\frac{1}{2}$ teaspoon sea salt and remaining 1 teaspoon lemon juice.

4. Chill immediately in a covered container. Aioli will keep for several days in the refrigerator.

Variation: For a Spanish twist, add 1 teaspoon smoked Spanish paprika.

PRIME CUT

You can purchase prepared garlic paste, but it's easy to make your own. Simply finely chop fresh garlic cloves, add a pinch of salt, and grind it to a paste with a mortar and pestle or use a knife to crush and grind it against a cutting board.

Homemade Ketchup

Homemade ketchup tastes of sweet tomato goodness. This homemade version is better than anything you can get out of a bottle.

Yield:	Cook time:	Marinate time:	Serving size:
about 20 ounces	1 hour 45 minutes	2 hours	1 tablespoon

1 (28-oz.) can whole tomatoes in purée

2 TB. olive oil

1 medium onion, chopped

1 TB. tomato paste

¾ cup packed dark brown sugar

½ cup cider vinegar

1 tsp. garlic powder

¼ tsp. ground allspice

¼ tsp. ground clove

1 tsp. kosher salt

1. Pour entire can of tomatoes, including sauce, into a blender. Purée until smooth, adding 2 tablespoons water if necessary to achieve smooth consistency.

2. Heat olive oil in a heavy 4-quart saucepan over moderate heat. Add onion and cook, stirring often, about 8 minutes or until softened.

3. Add puréed tomatoes, tomato paste, dark brown sugar, cider vinegar, garlic powder, allspice, clove, and kosher salt. Reduce heat to low and simmer for an hour, uncovered, until very thick, stirring occasionally.

4. Remove from heat and cool for 15 to 20 minutes.

5. Pour half of mixture into a blender and blend until smooth. Remove to a storage container and repeat with second half of mixture.

6. Chill, covered, for at least 2 hours before serving to allow flavors to develop. Ketchup keeps for several days in the refrigerator.

CHEF'S CHOICE

To make a spicier ketchup, add ½ teaspoon cayenne. You can use this ketchup as the base for homemade barbecue or cocktail sauce.

King Family BBQ Sauce

This is a sweet and very smoky barbecue sauce that has a kick of acidity.

Yield:	Cook time:	Serving size:
5 cups	40 minutes	1 tablespoon

¼ cup plus 2 TB. packed dark
   brown sugar

½ cup cider vinegar

¼ cup molasses

¼ cup honey (optional)

¼ cup Worcestershire sauce

2 TB. prepared yellow mustard

2 TB. liquid smoke

4 tsp. chili powder

2 tsp. freshly ground black pepper

2 tsp. garlic powder

1 tsp. ground allspice

¼ tsp. ground cloves

4 cups ketchup

1. Combine dark brown sugar, cider vinegar, molasses, honey (if using), Worcestershire sauce, prepared yellow mustard, liquid smoke, chili powder, black pepper, garlic powder, allspice, and cloves in a large, deep, heavy, nonreactive saucepan and bring to a simmer over medium heat.

2. Cook, uncovered, until ingredients are dissolved, stirring constantly, about 5 minutes.

3. Add ketchup and bring to a boil, stirring well, as ketchup has a tendency to spatter.

4. Reduce the heat slightly and gently simmer sauce, uncovered, until dark, thick, and richly flavored, about 30 minutes, stirring often.

5. Use immediately or transfer to jars, cool to room temperature, cover, and refrigerate. The sauce will keep for several months.

CHEF'S CHOICE

For a spicier sauce, add 2 or more teaspoons cayenne pepper in step 1.

Horseradish Cream Sauce

This creamy sauce has a spicy taste of horseradish.

Yield:	Prep time:	Serving size:
about 1 pint	10 minutes	1 tablespoon

1 pt. sour cream

3 TB. prepared horseradish or to taste

¼ tsp. salt or to taste

½ tsp. black pepper or to taste

2 tsp. red wine vinegar

1. In a small bowl, combine sour cream, horseradish, salt, black pepper, and red wine vinegar.

2. Taste and adjust seasoning.

3. Serve immediately, or store in a covered container in the refrigerator until it's ready to serve. This cream sauce will keep for several days in the refrigerator.

CHEF'S CHOICE

This sauce pairs well with beef sausages as well as beef roasts and steaks. It also can be added to mashed potatoes in small quantities to give them a kick. Mix the sauce with equal parts homemade catsup for a pinky horseradish sauce, which is perfect for dipping with tater tots, shrimp, or fries.

Cocktail Sauce

This is a recipe from Paul Lindemuth, owner and chef of The Art of Food. This fresh-tasting sauce goes great with mixed seafood sausage.

Yield:	Prep time:	Serving size:
about 3 cups	10 minutes	1 teaspoon

1½ cups ketchup

1½ cups chili sauce

Freshly squeezed juice of 2 lemons

3 to 4 TB. prepared horseradish or to taste

1. In a small bowl, combine ketchup, chili sauce, lemon juice, and horseradish.

2. Chill in a covered container in the refrigerator until it's ready to serve. Cocktail sauce will last several days in the refrigerator.

CHEF'S CHOICE

This cocktail sauce is so simple to make and delicious you will never need to buy cocktail sauce again! It tastes great with boiled shrimp, crab cakes, and even seafood pasta salads.

Caramelized Onions

Sweet, succulent, and juicy, these onions taste amazing by themselves, but they also are a perfect accompaniment to your homemade sausages.

Yield:	Prep time:	Cook time:	Serving size:
1 pint	15 minutes	25 minutes	1 large spoonful

Olive oil, vegetable oil, or butter

2 lb. Spanish onions, or any other yellow or white onion, sliced

1 tsp. sea salt or to taste

1 tsp. black pepper or to taste

1. In a large sauté pan over high heat, add enough olive oil to coat bottom of the pan.

2. When olive oil is hot, add Spanish onions and reduce heat to medium.

3. Season with sea salt and black pepper.

4. Stir occasionally to avoid burning, but be careful to avoid overmixing, which can mush onions. Sauté for 15 to 20 minutes, or until tender and golden. Remove onions from heat and allow to cool.

5. Serve immediately or refrigerate for up to 5 days.

CHEF'S CHOICE

The next time you make homemade onion soup, use this recipe as a base. Combine it with homemade beef or pork stock and top it with Gruyere cheese and croutons.

Sautéed Peppers and Onions

These sweet and juicy vegetables are just right for topping your Italian sausages.

Yield:	Prep time:	Cook time:	Serving size:
1 pint	15 minutes	25 minutes	1 large spoonful

Olive oil or vegetable oil

3 large red and/or green bell peppers, seeded, cored, and sliced

1 large Spanish onion, or any other yellow or white onion, sliced

1 tsp. sea salt or to taste

1 tsp. black pepper or to taste

1. In a large sauté pan over high heat, add enough olive oil to coat bottom of the pan.

2. When olive oil is hot, add bell peppers and Spanish onion, and season with sea salt and black pepper. Cook for 7 to 10 minutes, tossing bell peppers and onion often to avoid burning, and then reduce heat to low and cook for another 5 minutes. Remove to a medium bowl to cool.

3. Serve immediately or refrigerate for up to 5 days.

CHEF'S CHOICE

You can add 1 teaspoon oregano or other herb blend to give these vegetables flavors to match the rest of your meal. If you're serving the vegetables with Italian sausage, try using an Italian herb mix. For a French twist, add 1 teaspoon herbes de Provence or a blend of dried thyme, rosemary, and tarragon.

White Pork Stock

Pork stock makes a great base for just about any soup. It contains almost no calories, but it gives a richness to soups and sauces that's impossible to get from bouillon or powdered broths.

Yield:	Cook time:	Serving size:
1 gallon	4–6 hours	1 cup

4 pork shoulder bones

1 bay leaf

4 whole black peppercorns or pinch of ground black pepper

5 qt. water

1 large yellow onion, peeled and cut into 8 pieces

3 ribs celery, washed and cut into thirds

3 large carrots, washed and cut into thirds

1. Put pork bones, bay leaf, and black peppercorns in an 8-quart stockpot. Add water and bring to a simmer over high heat. Reduce heat to medium-low and simmer for 3 hours.

2. Add yellow onion, celery, and carrots to stock. Add additional water to cover vegetables if necessary. Continue to simmer for 1 hour.

3. Move pot to a cool burner or to your countertop to cool for 30 minutes.

4. Remove and discard bones and vegetables. Strain stock thought a cheesecloth-lined colander into a second pan or large bowl. Use immediately or refrigerate for up to 3 days for later use.

CHEF'S CHOICE

For additional flavor, add your favorite herbs and spices such as tarragon and oregano in step 1. Make sure to only use spices that will enhance the dishes for which you will use the stock. Adding ¼ teaspoon Spanish smoked paprika and 2 whole cloves garlic makes a great base for a vegetable soup.

Making a Meal of Your Sausages

In This Chapter

- Adding sausages to sauces, dips, and gravies
- Using sausages in casseroles and entrées
- Building better hot dogs, coney dogs, and brats

A delectable homemade, artisan sausage can be as complex and as nuanced as a finished dish and, as such, it can be one of the best ingredients to add to your cooking. You can incorporate sausages into quiches, add them to appetizers, and showcase them as the main entrée.

This chapter features recipes—including such favorites as cassoulet, biscuits and gravy, and paella—for cooking with your artisan sausages. It also shows you how to build a better Chicago hotdog, Detroit Coney dog, and Wisconsin brat.

Honey Chorizo Spread

This is an absolutely addictive tapas dish. The savory chorizo is accentuated by the sweet honey.

Yield:	Prep time:	Cook time:	Serving size:
About ¾ cup	5 minutes	8 minutes	1–2 tablespoons

2 links uncooked chorizo (see Chapter 9)

⅓ cup honey

1. Add enough water to a medium saucepan to fill it three quarters of the way, add chorizo, and bring water to a boil over medium-high heat. Reduce heat, and cook until sausages are poached or about 15 minutes, turning the sausages over after 10 minutes. Remove links to cool 2 minutes. Slice into ¼-inch slices.

2. In a food processor fitted with a standard blade, chop chorizo and honey for 5 minutes or until chunky but well combined. Refrigerate for at least 1 hour. Serve with crackers or bread.

CHEF'S CHOICE

Your choice of chorizo has a big impact on this dish's flavor profile. Colombian Chorizo adds a distinctive cumin note, Fresh Portuguese Linguisa leaves a spicy aftertaste, and Argentinian Chorizo lends this dish the richness of bacon.

Chorizo Empanadas

This rich and savory dish makes a great appetizer.

Yield:	Prep time:	Cook time:	Serving size:
18 empanadas	20 minutes	20 minutes	1 empanada

3 oz. chorizo (about 1½ links), cooked and decased (see Chapter 9)

¼ cup raisins

½ cup pitted kalamata or black olives

1 hardboiled egg

3 TB. tomato sauce

1 TB. sherry wine

½ tsp. oregano

½ tsp. Spanish smoked paprika

Sea salt

Ground black pepper

2 sheets prepared puff pastry dough, thawed

1 egg, beaten

1. Preheat oven to 350°F. Put chorizo, raisins, kalamata olives, hardboiled egg, tomato sauce, sherry wine, oregano, Spanish smoked paprika, sea salt, and black pepper in a food processor fitted with a standard blade. Chop for 2 minutes or until fine.

2. Cut 9 circles, 4 inches in diameter, from each sheet of puff pastry. Put 1 rounded teaspoon of meat mixture in the middle of each circle. Fold over circle. Pinch ends together and crimp with fingers or fork to look attractive. Brush with egg. Set on nonstick cookie sheet.

3. Bake in oven for 20 minutes or until lightly browned. Serve with garlic mayonnaise.

CHEF'S CHOICE

If you can't find puff pastry dough in your grocer's frozen foods section, you can substitute thawed crescent roll dough pressed flat with a rolling pin. Use two 8-ounce cans.

Italian Sausage Tomato Sauce

This rich tomato sauce brims with spices and is perfect for topping spaghetti, lasagna, and other Italian pastas.

Yield:	Prep time:	Cook time:	Serving size:
7–8 cups	20 minutes	1½ hours	½ cup

Olive oil

1½ lb. Italian Bulk Sausage (see Chapter 5)

1 medium onion, chopped

6 cloves garlic, minced

26 oz. can crushed tomatoes

6 oz. can tomato paste

1 cup dry red wine, such as Chianti

1 TB. sugar

2 tsp. dried Italian seasoning blend

1 tsp. ground black pepper

Sea salt

3 TB. fresh basil, chopped

Grated Italian cheese

1. Warm olive oil in a medium pot over medium-high heat for 1 minute. Add Italian Bulk Sausage and sauté for 8 minutes or until cooked through. Use a wooden spoon to break sausage into small pieces as it cooks. Reduce heat to medium, add onion and garlic, and sauté for 5 minutes or until translucent.

2. Add tomatoes, tomato paste, dry red wine, sugar, Italian seasoning blend, black pepper, and sea salt. Reduce heat to low and simmer for at least 45 minutes. Add 2 tablespoons fresh basil and cook for another 15 minutes.

3. Serve over fresh pasta and garnish with remaining 1 tablespoon basil and grated Italian cheese.

CHEF'S CHOICE

Two great, grate-able Italian cheeses are Parmigiano Reggiano and Grana Padano.

Sausage Stuffing

This is a great stuffing to use for Thanksgiving.

Yield:	Prep time:	Cook time:	Serving size:
10 cups	30 minutes	30 minutes	½ cup

1 lb. Bulk Breakfast Sausage or Italian Bulk Sausage (see Chapter 5)

1 medium yellow onion, diced

3 ribs celery, diced

2 medium apples, cored and diced

½ cup raisins

8 cups French bread cubes

1 TB. fresh parsley, chopped

1 TB. fresh sage, chopped

1 egg, lightly beaten

¼ cup unsalted butter, melted

½ cup low salt chicken or turkey stock

Sea salt

Ground black pepper

Unsalted butter or vegetable oil

1. Preheat oven to 325°F. In a large saucepan over medium high heat, sauté Bulk Breakfast Sausage for 8 minutes or until cooked, using a wooden spoon to break up the sausage as it is cooked. Add yellow onion, celery, apples, and raisins, cook for another 3 to 5 minutes or until just beginning to turn translucent. Drain off excess fat. Set aside.

2. In a large bowl, mix French bread cubes with parsley and sage. Add sausage mixture and egg and mix with a wooden spoon. Add melted butter and chicken stock a couple tablespoons at a time. If mixture is quite moist, don't add so much butter or stock. If it's still a bit dry, add more stock, 1 tablespoon at a time. Season with sea salt and black pepper.

3. Grease a large, covered casserole dish with unsalted butter or vegetable oil. Transfer mixture to casserole dish and bake covered for 30 minutes, then remove cover and cook uncovered for 10 to 15 minutes or until golden brown. Or stuff in a turkey or chicken and bake as instructed.

CHEF'S CHOICE

This stuffing tastes great when made with crumbly cornbread. Use about ½ breadcrumbs and ½ cornbread.

Sausage Gravy

Sausage gravy is often referred to as "country" or "white" gravy. This creamy, savory Southern specialty is perfect for breakfast. This recipe is from Andrew Waszak, a business partner and cooking buddy of Jeff.

Yield:	Prep time:	Cook time:	Serving size:
1½ quarts	5 minutes	40 minutes	½ cup gravy

1 lb. Bulk Breakfast Sausage (see Chapter 5)

¾ cup. white or whole-wheat flour

4 cups 2 percent milk

1½ tsp. salt (or to taste)

½ tsp. ground black pepper (or to taste)

Pinch cayenne (or to taste)

1. Heat a large, high-sided sauté pan over medium to medium-high heat for 1 minute. Add enough vegetable oil to coat the bottom of the pan. (If you're using leaner breakfast sausage, you can add more oil.)

2. Add Bulk Breakfast Sausage and, using a wooden spoon, break into small pieces. Cook for 5 to 8 minutes or until meat is thoroughly brown.

3. Add white flour to pan and mix until no clumps remain. Cook for 3 to 5 minutes or until flour turns golden brown.

4. Add milk and season with salt, black pepper, and cayenne. Stir often, until milk thickens, about 10 to 15 minutes.

5. Reduce heat to medium-low and simmer for about 10 minutes to fully develop flavor. Taste and adjust seasoning.

6. Serve this gravy over freshly baked biscuits, chicken fried steak, or ham and eggs. You can store in sealed container for up to 3 days in the refrigerator or for several months in the freezer.

CHEF'S CHOICE

If you're in a pinch and are using store-bought sausage, try adding ½ teaspoon poultry seasoning and ⅛ teaspoon garlic powder to boost the flavor.

Jambalaya

This Louisiana favorite sings with spice, seafood, and sausage. It's a crowd-pleaser recipe adapted from Pat and Ron Rewers.

Yield:	Prep time:	Cook time:	Serving size:
8 servings	30 minutes	30 minutes	1 large bowl

10 oz. medium shrimp, peeled, deveined

10 oz. chicken breast, diced

8 oz. Tasso Ham, or substitute other smoked ham, diced

½ tsp. cayenne (or to taste)

1½ tsp. kosher salt

1½ tsp. ground white pepper

1 tsp. dried thyme leaves

½ tsp. ground black pepper

¼ tsp. sage

2 TB. extra-virgin olive oil

1 cup onion, chopped

½ cup green bell pepper, chopped

½ cup celery, chopped

2 TB. garlic, finely chopped

½ cup chopped fresh tomatoes

3 bay leaves

1 tsp. Worcestershire sauce

1 tsp. Louisiana-style hot sauce (or to taste)

1 TB. brown sugar

¾ cup medium or long-grain white rice

3 cups chicken stock

10 oz. Andouille Sausage (see Chapter 14), sliced into ½ inch rounds

1. In a medium bowl combine shrimp, chicken, Tasso Ham, cayenne, kosher salt, white pepper, thyme, black pepper, and sage. Use your hands to work in the seasoning and set aside.

2. In a large pan over medium-high heat, add extra-virgin olive oil, onion, green bell pepper, and celery and sauté for 3 minutes.

3. Add garlic, tomatoes, bay leaves, Worcestershire sauce, hot sauce, and brown sugar. Stir in white rice and slowly add chicken stock. Reduce heat to medium and cook until rice absorbs liquid and becomes tender, stirring occasionally, about 15 minutes.

4. When rice is just tender, add shrimp and chicken mixture and Andouille Sausage. Cook until meat is cooked through, about 10 minutes. Adjust seasoning with additional kosher salt and black pepper if necessary.

Variation: If you want to make this dish a bit more healthy, substitute brown rice for white rice, add 1 cup of stock, and increase cooking time to 40 minutes.

PRIME CUT

This Creole dish originated in New Orleans, and it's believed to have started out as a version of Spanish paella.

Red Beans and Rice

This is a hearty but simple dish with a little bit of a kick that won't overwhelm you with spiciness.

Yield:	Prep time:	Cook time:	Serving size:
8 bowls	12 hours	2½ hours	1 medium bowl

1 lb. red beans

1 ham hock (optional)

7 cups water

1 bay leaf

1 large onion, chopped

3 ribs celery, chopped

1 green bell pepper, chopped

1 clove garlic, finely chopped

2 tsp. Cajun spice mix from Andouille Sausage recipe (see Chapter 14), or a pinch each of black pepper and cayenne pepper to taste

½–1 lb. Andouille Sausage (see Chapter 14), sliced into ½-inch rounds

½ tsp. sea salt (or to taste)

6 cups cooked long- or medium-grain white rice

1. Rinse red beans then place in large bowl or pot. Add enough water to cover beans by a couple inches. Soak beans overnight at room temperature.

2. Rinse and drain soaked beans. In a large pot (such as a 5-quart Dutch oven) over high heat, add ham hock (if using), water, and bay leaf. Bring water to a boil, then reduce heat to medium-low and simmer, stirring occasionally, for 1½ hours or until beans are tender.

3. Add onion, celery, green bell pepper, garlic, and Cajun spice mix. Continue to simmer for 30 minutes, stirring occasionally. Add more water if it gets too thick.

4. Add Andouille Sausage and sea salt. Continue simmering for 30 minutes. Serve over hot white rice.

CHEF'S CHOICE

This dish tastes even better if you refrigerate it overnight, and reheat it the following day. Store beans and rice separately to maintain texture of the rice.

Cassoulet

This savory French casserole is a hearty, stick-to-your-bones meat dish.

Yield:	Prep time:	Cook time:	Serving size:
8 servings	20 minutes	60 minutes	1 large bowl

1 TB. butter

1 clove garlic, finely chopped

2 cups panko breadcrumbs

10 oz. any mild fresh or smoked linked sausage, such as Fresh Polish Kielbasa (see Chapter 8) or Smoked Polish Sausage (see Chapter 14)

10 oz. boneless, skinless duck breasts

1 medium yellow onion, roughly chopped

2 medium carrots, diced

2 ribs celery, diced

2 tsp. garlic, finely chopped

2 cans (15 oz. each) cannellini beans or other white beans, rinsed

2 cans (14.5 oz. each) fire-roasted diced tomatoes, with juice

2 TB. tomato paste

1 cup chicken stock

2 tsp. fresh thyme, finely chopped

1 tsp. fresh rosemary, finely chopped

2 TB. Parmesan cheese, grated

2 TB. fresh parsley, chopped

1. Melt butter in a sauté pan on medium heat. Add garlic and cook until translucent, about 3 minutes. (Do not allow garlic to burn. If it does burn, discard, wash pan, and start over.) Add panko breadcrumbs and mix with wooden spoon until butter coats breadcrumbs evenly. Cook, stirring often, for 7 to 10 minutes or until golden brown. Remove to a bowl to cool.

2. In a large pot over medium-high heat, add enough olive oil to coat the bottom. Add sausage links and brown on all sides, about 8 minutes. Remove sausage to cutting board to cool.

3. In same pot, brown duck breasts, 4 to 6 minutes per side. Remove to cutting board to cool.

4. In same pot, add yellow onion, carrots, and celery, reduce heat to medium, then add garlic. Sauté for 5 minutes or until lightly browned.

5. Add cannellini beans, tomatoes with their juice, tomato paste, chicken stock, thyme, and rosemary to pot and bring to a simmer. Reduce heat to medium-low and simmer for 20 minutes, gently stirring occasionally.

6. While beans and tomatoes are simmering, cut sausage into $\frac{1}{2}$-inch thick rounds and duck into bite-sized pieces.

7. Mix cooled breadcrumbs with Parmesan cheese and parsley.

8. Add sausage and duck to the tomato and bean mixture and stir with a wooden spoon. Spread breadcrumb mixture on top of cassoulet and simmer for 10 to 15 minutes. Serve as a one-pot dinner or as a main course.

CHEF'S CHOICE

For a crisp top, finish cooking last step in a preheated 350°F oven. This dish pairs well with a Côtes du Rhône or other Syrah-based wine.

Paella

Flavors of saffron, seafood, and sausage mingle in this Spanish dish, which tastes great with a brut (dry) Spanish cava or sparkling wine. The recipe is from Paul Lindemuth, owner and chef of The Art of Food catering company in the Chicagoland area.

Yield:	Prep time:	Cook time:	Serving size:
10–12 bowls	30 minutes	75 minutes	1 large bowl

$\frac{1}{4}$ cup fresh oregano, finely chopped

$\frac{1}{4}$ cup fresh thyme, finely chopped

$\frac{1}{4}$ cup fresh Italian parsley, finely chopped

$\frac{3}{4}$ cup. olive oil

8 TB. dry red wine, such as Spanish Rioja

1 TB. ground black pepper

1 TB. ground coriander

8 large cloves garlic, finely chopped

1 tsp. cayenne

2 TB. sea salt

1 tsp. red wine vinegar

8 chicken thighs

2 lbs. Fresh Portuguese Linguisa (see Chapter 9), Fresh Spanish Chorizo (see Chapter 9), or Fresh Polish Kielbasa (see Chapter 8), cut into 1-inch pieces

4 large onions, coarsely chopped

28 oz. can diced fire-roasted tomatoes, drained

8 oz. ham steak, $\frac{1}{2}$ inch thick, cut into 1 inch strips

$6\frac{1}{2}$ cups low-sodium chicken broth

1 tsp. saffron threads

4 cups short-grain white rice

2 lb. large shrimp, peeled (tails left intact) and deveined

1 lb. halibut filets, cut into 1-inch pieces

3 large red bell peppers, stems removed, seeded and cut in half

3 large yellow bell peppers, stems removed, seeded and cut in half

3 large green bell peppers, stems removed, seeded and cut in half

10 oz. frozen peas, thawed

2 lemons, cut into wedges for garnish

1. In a small bowl combine oregano, thyme, and Italian parsley. Transfer half the herbs to the work bowl of a food processor fitted with a standard steel blade. Add $\frac{1}{4}$ cup olive oil, 1 tablespoon dry red wine, black pepper, coriander, 3 cloves garlic, cayenne, sea salt, and red wine vinegar. Process until a coarse paste forms.

2. Place chicken thighs on a large plate. Rub all but 2 tablespoons of herb paste over the chicken. Cover and refrigerate chicken until ready to use. Reserve the remaining herb paste.

3. Pour 2 tablespoons olive oil into each of two large casserole dishes that are safe to use on the stovetop, or use large sauté or paella pans. Warm over medium heat. Divide Fresh Portuguese Linguisa, onions, tomatoes, ham, remaining chopped herbs, and remaining 5 cloves garlic between the casseroles. Cook over medium heat until the onions are soft and golden brown, about 15 minutes. Transfer the mixture to a large bowl.

4. Pour 2 tablespoons remaining olive oil into each of the casseroles. Add half of the chicken to each casserole and sauté over medium heat until brown, turning frequently, about 8 to 10 minutes. Transfer the chicken to a plate.

5. While chicken is cooking, add chicken broth and saffron to a large saucepan and simmer over medium heat.

6. Return half of onion and sausage mixture to each of the casserole dishes. Add half of white rice to each of the casseroles. Cook over high heat until opaque, stirring frequently, about 5 to 7 minutes.

7. Divide remaining herb paste and remaining 7 tablespoons of wine between the casseroles. Bring to a simmer, scraping up any brown bits. Stir half of the stock mixture into each casserole. Bring to a boil, then reduce the heat, cover, and simmer for 15 minutes.

8. Divide shrimp and halibut pieces between casseroles. Cover and continue cooking until rice is tender and seafood is cooked through, about 10 minutes.

9. While paella is cooking, prepare a medium-hot charcoal fire or preheat a stovetop grill pan.

10. Add sautéed chicken to the grill and cook until it is cooked through, turning occasionally, about 10 minutes. Transfer to a platter. Cover with foil and keep warm.

11. Grill red bell peppers, yellow bell peppers, and green bell peppers until they are brown in spots, turning frequently, about 10 minutes. When they are cool enough to handle, cut bell peppers into $1/2$-inch strips.

12. Divide chicken, bell peppers, and peas between casseroles. Cover casseroles and remove them from the heat. Allow paella to stand for 15 minutes.

13. Serve garnished with lemon wedges.

PRIME CUT

Paella, considered the national dish of Spain, hails from Valencia. Many different versions of paella, using different fish, seafood, and meats, have evolved over the years—there's even a version using pasta instead of rice.

Italian Stuffed Peppers

This simple and quick recipe boasts traditional Italian flavors, and it's perfect for a weeknight supper.

Yield:	Prep time:	Cook time:	Serving size:
4 peppers	15 minutes	60 minutes	1 pepper

4 medium green peppers

1 lb. Italian Bulk Sausage (see Chapter 5) or any other bulk sausage

1 egg

¼ cup breadcrumbs

2 cups tomato pasta sauce

½ cup grated mozzarella cheese

1. Preheat oven to 350°F.

2. Cut off top of green peppers and remove seeds and as much of the white flesh as possible. Trim just enough of the bottom of each pepper so that it stands without tipping, but be careful not to cut open a hole.

3. In a medium bowl, mix Italian Bulk Sausage with egg and breadcrumbs until combined.

4. Stuff sausage mixture into peppers.

5. Pour tomato pasta sauce into a medium-sized baking pan.

6. Stand peppers upright in sauce and sprinkle mozzarella cheese evenly over their tops.

7. Bake for 50 to 60 minutes or until peppers are tender and sausage is cooked through.

CHEF'S CHOICE

To add a little more flavor, add 2 tablespoons fresh herbs such as basil, parsley, or thyme. You can also substitute 1 to 2 cups cooked rice for the breadcrumbs.

Spanish Stuffed Peppers

This is a more exotic riff on the preceding Italian Stuffed Peppers recipe.

Yield:	Prep time:	Cook time:	Serving size:
6 pepper boats	15 minutes	25 minutes	1 or 2 pepper boats

3 sweet pointed peppers, Italian sweet peppers, or other sweet peppers

1 lb. fresh sausage, such as Columbian Chorizo (see Chapter 9)

1 egg

¼ cup breadcrumbs

12 slices Urgelia cheese

¼ cup dry white wine such as Albariño

2 TB. water

1. Preheat oven to 350°F.

2. Cut off top of sweet pointed peppers, cut in half lengthwise, and remove seeds and as much of the white flesh as possible.

3. In a medium bowl, mix sausage with egg and breadcrumbs until combined.

4. Press sausage mixture into pepper halves.

5. Place Urgelia cheese over peppers so it covers them entirely and hangs over edges.

6. Pour dry white wine and water into baking pan. Place peppers in braising liquid and cover pan with foil.

7. Bake for 12 minutes. Uncover and bake for another 5 minutes or until peppers are tender and sausage is cooked through.

CHEF'S CHOICE

Urgelia is a semi-soft, buttery cow's milk cheese from Spain. If you can't find it, you can substitute with Mahon (another type of mild Spanish cheese), Provolone, or Gouda.

English Sausage Rolls

This traditional English appetizer is what Americans often call "pigs in a blanket." Buttery puff pastry encapsulates savory sausage links.

Yield:	Prep time:	Cook time:	Serving size:
36 small or 18 large rolls	60 minutes	30 minutes	4 small or 2 large rolls

1 egg

1 TB. water

1 (2-sheet) pack puff pastry, thawed

1–1½ lb. bangers (see Chapter 10) or other mild sausage, bulk or removed from casings

1. Preheat oven to 375°F.

2. In a small bowl, beat egg and water with a fork and then set aside.

3. Cut each sheet of puff pastry into two even pieces.

4. Divide bangers into four portions.

5. Spread each sausage portion into an even strip centered across the length of each piece of dough.

6. Roll dough around sausage. Pinch and smooth seam.

7. Cut into 1-inch pieces for bite-sized appetizers or 2-inch pieces for larger appetizers.

8. Place a sheet of parchment paper on a baking sheet. Line rolls on parchment paper, seam side down. Brush tops of rolls with egg. Make two diagonal scores on each roll.

9. Bake for 25 to 30 minutes or until puff pastry browns and sausage is cooked.

Variation: To make a cheesy version of this appetizer, mix ¼ cup grated cheddar cheese into the sausage in step 4.

PRIME CUT

This popular English dish was served at Prince William's wedding. While Americans would call this "pigs in a blanket," if you order "pigs in a blanket" in Great Britain, you'll get sausages wrapped in bacon.

How to Build a Better: Chicago-Style Hot Dog

In the Midwest, the perfect hot dog is served without ketchup. Serve with piping hot French fries for the perfect All-American meal.

Yield:	Prep time:	Cook time:	Serving size:
1 sausage	10 minutes	30 minutes	1 link

1 poppy seed bun

1 steamed All-American Hot Dog (see Chapter 10); can also be reheated in simmering water

Yellow mustard, to taste

1 TB. chopped onion

Relish, to taste

2 sport or Tabasco peppers (optional)

2 slices tomato

1 spear dill pickle

1 dash celery salt (optional)

1. Lightly steam bun, or microwave for 20 to 30 seconds, just until heated through.

2. Place All-American Hot Dog in bun. Top with yellow mustard, onion, relish, sport peppers (if using), tomato, dill pickle, and celery salt (if using).

CHEF'S CHOICE

A great, simplified version of a Chicago Style uses only mustard, onion, relish, and peppers with the addition of a handful of fries right on top. This is how Gene & Jude's, an internationally known hot dog stand, has been making their hot dogs for more than 60 years.

How to Build a Better: Wisconsin-Style Brat

No Wisconsin barbecue is complete without brats, and the perfect brat is served German-style.

Yield:	Prep time:	Cook time:	Serving size:
1 sausage	10 minutes	30 minutes	1 link

1 brat or sausage roll

1 link Basic German Bratwurst (see Chapter 6), poached and grilled

Düsseldorf or Dijon mustard

1 TB. sauerkraut (or to taste), drained and rinsed

1 TB. chopped raw onion

1. Lightly steam roll, or microwave for 20 to 30 seconds, just until heated through.

2. Place Basic German Bratwurst in roll and top with Düsseldorf mustard, sauerkraut, and onion.

CHEF'S CHOICE

For a cheesy touch, add ½ cup grated Wisconsin cheddar cheese. You can also replace the raw onion with 2 tablespoons caramelized onions.

How to Build a Better: Polish Sausage

Very similar to building a brat, the only difference is the mustard.

Yield:	Prep time:	Cook time:	Serving size:
1 sausage	10 minutes	30 minutes	1 link

1 hot dog bun or sausage roll

1 link Fresh Polish Kielbasa (see Chapter 8) or Smoked Polish Sausage (see Chapter 14), poached and grilled

Yellow mustard

1 TB. sauerkraut, drained and rinsed

2 TB. caramelized onions

1. Lightly steam bun, or microwave for 20 to 30 seconds, just until heated through.

2. Place Fresh Polish Kielbasa in bun and top with yellow mustard, sauerkraut, and caramelized onions.

CHEF'S CHOICE

If you don't like sauerkraut, try sweet and sour cabbage instead.

How to Build a Better: Italian Sausage

Peppers, onions, cheese, and tomato sauce all top a perfect Italian sausage.

Yield:	Prep time:	Cook time:	Serving size:
1 sausage	10 minutes	30 minutes	1 link

1 sausage roll or 6-inch section of baguette, cut open like a bun

1 link any style Italian sausage (see Chapter 7), grilled or sautéed

2 to 3 TB. sautéed peppers and onions or to taste

2 TB. marinara sauce

¼ cup mozzarella cheese, grated

1. Lightly steam roll, or microwave for 20 to 30 seconds, just until heated through.

2. Place sausage in roll and top with peppers and onions, marinara sauce, and mozzarella cheese.

CHEF'S CHOICE

For added kick, add 2 teaspoons hot or mild giardiniera, which is an Italian relish made with pickled vegetables.

How to Build a Better: Game Sausage

Game sausages are intensely flavored, so the perfect grilled game sausage should be matched with the strong flavors of onion, horseradish mustard, and cheese.

Yield:	Prep time:	Cook time:	Serving size:
1 sausage	10 minutes	30 minutes	1 link

1 sausage roll

1 link venison or other game sausage (see Chapter 13)

Strong mustard, such as horseradish or stone ground

1 TB. chopped raw onion

¼ cup grated or crumbled strong cheese, such as sharp cheddar or blue

1. Lightly steam roll, or microwave for 20 to 30 seconds, just until heated through.

2. Place sausage in roll and top with mustard, onion, and cheese.

CHEF'S CHOICE

Feel free to substitute other intensely flavored condiments and toppings. Try brick cheese instead of cheddar or blue cheese; BBQ sauce or horseradish cream instead of mustard; or 2 tablespoons caramelized onions instead of raw onions.

How to Build a Better: Detroit Coney Dog

This special chili dog has quite a kick.

Yield:	Prep time:	Cook time:	Serving size:
2 quarts sauce; 1 sausage	10 minutes (sauce); 10 minutes (sausage)	6 to 10 hours (sauce); 30 minutes (sausage)	$\frac{1}{3}$ cup; 1 link

½ cup lard or shortening

2 lb. ground beef (90 percent lean)

½ lb. beef heart, finely ground

2 cups chicken or beef stock, or water

3 TB. butter

3 TB. flour

2 TB. chili powder

2 TB. Spanish hot paprika

2 TB. prepared yellow mustard plus to taste

1 TB. cumin powder

1 TB. turmeric

2 tsp. garlic powder

2 tsp. onion powder

1 tsp. salt

½ tsp. dried oregano

1 hot dog bun

1 All-American Hot Dog (see Chapter 10)

2 TB. chopped yellow onion

1. Melt lard in large pot over medium to medium-high heat. Add beef and beef heart to lard and mash into small pieces as meat browns, about 7 to 10 minutes.

2. Add chicken stock to pot. When it comes to a light boil, reduce heat to medium-low and simmer for 20 minutes.

3. While main pot simmers, make roux: in a medium pan, melt butter over medium heat. Reduce heat to medium-low and add flour, stirring almost constantly until golden brown, about 10 to 15 minutes.

4. Add roux, chili powder, Spanish hot paprika, yellow mustard, cumin powder, turmeric, garlic powder, onion powder, salt, and oregano. Mix well to combine.

5. Reduce heat to low and simmer, covered, for 3 to 7 hours, stirring occasionally to prevent burning. Uncover and continue simmering for 3 hours to thicken to desired consistency. If sauce gets too thick, add water to thin as necessary.

6.. Lightly steam bun, or microwave for 20 to 30 seconds, just until heated through.

7. Place All-American Hot Dog in bun and top with ⅓ cup sauce, yellow onion, and yellow mustard.

Variation: If you don't like the idea of eating beef hearts, just replace with ground beef.

PRIME CUT

Coney Island chili sauce is beanless and tomatoless, and it's believed to have first been created in Detroit in 1914.

Cooking, Pairing, and Serving Your Sausages

In This Chapter

- Cooking methods for sausage
- Pairing sausage with beverages
- Pairing sausage with condiments and other foods
- Serving suggestions for sausage
- Entertaining with sausage

As fun as it is to make sausages, you can have even more fun cooking and entertaining with them.

Nothing tastes quite as good as a perfectly grilled bratwurst on a hot summer day. But did you know that to grill a brat perfectly, you should poach it—preferably in beer—first?

As many times as we've enjoyed that perfect brat, we've also experienced a less-than-satisfying link. That's because people tend to overcook sausages. Who wants a tough, dried-out piece of meat? Fortunately, if you've read this far, you already know how to link your own linguisa, and with a little finesse and practice, you'll soon be able to poach, sauté, and grill it to perfection.

Once you've cooked your sausages to your liking, you're going to want to eat them, of course. And we suggest eating them with specific wines, beers, and even teas that can enhance their flavors.

And after you've made a few great batches of homemade sausage, you're going to want to share them with family and friends. It's great fun to match your homemade sausages with homemade condiments, plate them artistically, and incorporate them into dishes.

How to Cook Homemade Sausage

Just as there are two main types of fresh sausage—bulk and linked—there are two primary ways to cook sausage: sautéing and poaching. Then, of course, there's grilling.

Cooking Bulk Sausage

For bulk sausage, the main cooking method is sautéing or pan frying, using a little bit of fat.

If you're planning to use the sausage in crumbled form—for tacos, sausage gravy, or stuffing peppers, for example—form the bulk sausage into a single large patty. If you're serving breakfast sausage or other individual servings of sausage, form smaller, individually portioned patties.

Heat a large pan over medium-high heat for 1 minute. Drizzle a little canola or olive oil in the pan. Although sausages contain fat in them, you will still need to add a little oil to get started. If you are cooking leaner sausage such as chicken or turkey sausage, you may want to add a little more oil. Let the oil warm for 1 minute and then add the patty or patties.

PRIME CUT

Heating the pan first—before you add oil or sausage—helps cook your food more quickly. It also helps to create a sear, which reduces the chance of the meat sticking to the pan.

Don't flip the sausage over immediately; instead, let it brown for a few minutes. Once the meat is nicely browned and sizzling, flip it over. Let it cook for a few more minutes until it is cooked through. Remove the patties and place them on a paper towel to drain and cool.

If you are sautéing it to crumble, after it is browned on one side, use your spatula or a wooden spoon to break it into chunks. Let the chunks cook for about 5 minutes, or until browned to your liking. Remove them from the pan and drain on a paper towel.

To grill bulk sausage patties, heat your grill to high heat first. Then add the patties and grill them on both sides until cooked through.

If you're sautéing or grilling leaner sausages like turkey and chicken, they tend to cook faster. You might also, in the case of sautéing, after browning them, add a tablespoon water or other liquid to the pan to poach them if they are not finished cooking when you sauté them. The main thing you want to watch with leaner sausages is that they do not get overcooked or dried out.

If you use a cooking thermometer, you want your pork or beef sausages to reach an internal temperature of 160°F. Poultry sausages should be cooked to 165°F.

> **THE GRIND**
>
> Although the USDA decreased the cooking temperature for whole cuts of pork—pork tenderloin, pork chops, and pork shoulder, for example—to 145°F, ground pork, including sausages, should be cooked to 160°F.

Cooking Fresh Sausage Links

When you cook fresh sausage links, you should first poach them and then finish cooking them on the grill or in a sauté pan. This two-pronged approach ensures that you don't burst the casings on the links and also that you fully cook the sausage without drying it out. If you just sautéd the links, you'd run the risk of drying them out or breaking the casing by the time they are fully cooked.

Grilling Fresh Sausage Links

Put the sausage links in a large pot half filled with water or another liquid and bring to a boil on high heat. Adding the sausage to the liquid before bringing it to a boil reduces the chance of bursting the casings.

> **PRIME CUT**
>
> Before placing your sausages in the poaching liquid, look them over carefully. If you see any air or fat pockets, prick a small hole in them with the tip of a knife. This prevents the pockets from bursting when the water temperature rises.

Once the water comes to a gentle boil, reduce the heat to medium to prevent it from reaching a rapid boil. Poach the sausages for 15 to 20 minutes. You can store the fully cooked sausages in the refrigerator for a couple of days before grilling.

To grill the sausages, preheat the grill to high heat. Place the sausages on the rack and cover the grill. Grill on one side for about 2 minutes, then turn them over to grill the other side for a minute or two, or until the desired level of char is reached. After grilling, let the sausages sit for a few minutes to cool slightly before serving.

Sautéing Fresh Sausage Links

To prepare your sausages for sautéing, first prick the casings where you see air or fat pockets to prevent them from bursting. Place the links in a large pan and add enough water to go about ¾ of the way up the links. Bring the water to a gentle boil on high heat.

Reduce the heat to medium to avoid the water reaching a rapid boil. Poach, covered, for 15 to 20 minutes, flipping sausages after 10 minutes.

Uncover the pan. If more than ⅛ inch of water remains in the pan, drain it. Otherwise just cook off the remaining liquid and brown the links thoroughly on all sides over medium-high heat. Add a drizzle of vegetable oil if the sausages don't render enough fat. Sauté for 5 to 8 minutes or until desired sear is reached.

THE GRIND

If you make your homemade sausages with collagen casings, pierce them more liberally with a knife before cooking. Collagen casings have more of a tendency to burst during the cooking process. A piercing every ¾ inch on both sides should prevent them from bursting.

When you are poaching sausages, add chopped onions, garlic, and/or fresh herbs to impart more flavor. After you poach the sausages, discard the onions, garlic, and herbs.

You can also cook or poach your sausages in sauces. For example, if you are cooking Italian sausage and plan to serve it with pasta and tomato sauce, poach the sausages in the tomato sauce for 20 to 30 minutes. The sausages add flavor to the sauce. For a little extra flavor, lightly sear the sausages in a sauté pan or char them on the grill before adding to the sauce.

You can poach sausages in water, broth, beer, wine, juice, or liquor. It doesn't have to be the most expensive beverage on the market, but it should be drinkable. A good rule of thumb: if you wouldn't drink it out of a can or bottle, then don't put it on your food. Usually a cheap beer or wine imparts a more imbalanced flavor to the meat because cheap beer and wine tend to have imbalanced flavors.

If you're planning to serve wine or beer with your sausages, then use this same drink to poach your sausages. Cooking your sausages in the same wine or beer (or liquor) that you're serving with your sausages helps ensure a satisfying pairing.

> **CHEF'S CHOICE**
>
> Bratwursts are traditionally poached in beer or a combination of half water and half beer. You can also poach kielbasa, chorizo, and other sausages in beer.

Beverage Pairing Strategies for Sausages

Beer goes with sausages the way peanut butter and jelly match up. This classic pairing works for sausages the world over, but not every beer matches perfectly with each sausage. Though you can certainly drink any beer with any sausage, to get the most out of both your sausage and your beer, try following some pairing strategies.

Goes With Where It Grows

The easiest pairing strategy is "goes with where it grows." This works for all types of cuisine, and it works with both beer and wine. Basically, cuisines and beverages of specific regions tend to enhance each other's flavors. A German brat, for example, goes great with a German beer. Or a Thai sausage with a Thai beer.

Use this strategy with nonalcoholic beverages, too. Serve a Chinese sausage with a Chinese oolong tea, for example. Or serve an Irish breakfast sausage with an Irish breakfast tea.

Logically, you can pair a sausage with a traditionally styled beverage, even if that beverage wasn't made in the same country of origin. For example, pair a brat with a German-style beer—even if that beer was made in Wisconsin. Or pair an Italian sausage with an Italian-style wine—even if the wine was produced in California.

Intensity with Intensity

You can pair sausages and beverages based on their level of intensity. Try matching a lighter sausage with a lighter beer or wine. For instance, a chicken sausage might taste great with a glass of sauvignon blanc. The delicate flavors of the sausage just sing with the crisp acidity of the wine. A fresh kielbasa tastes great with a pale ale, as the garlicky goodness of the sausage goes with the beer's hoppiness.

Pair heavier sausages—like venison, rabbit, and elk sausages—with darker beers and wines such as porters and stouts, Cabernet Sauvignon and Shiraz. In particular, the peppery bite and deep flavors of these sausages are enhanced by the intensity of these beers and wines.

The intensity rule has one big exception: don't pair hot, spicy sausages with dark wines and beers. Hot spices get hotter with darker wines and beers, making them more unpalatable. The tannins of wine or beer are intensified, creating almost a bitter taste, when paired with hot chiles. The alcohol content also intensifies with chiles.

Instead, pair hot or spicy foods with sweet beverages. A Mexican chorizo, made with spicy chilies, goes great with a sweet Riesling or Gewürztraminer or a fruity, citrusy lager.

THE GRIND

Always pair spicy sausages with sweeter beverages. This rule is especially important for wine pairings, because wine has more alcohol and tannins than beer.

Spicy sausages taste great with sweeter, nonalcoholic beverages, too, such as lemonade and sweet tea.

Matching Grilled and Smoked Sausages to Beverages

When pairing sausages with beverages, you will need to take into account how you cooked the sausages. When you grill a sausage, you're adding another dimension of flavor from the cooking process, and you need to take that extra flavor into account. If you grill a sausage, use slightly heavier wines or beers. The smoke from the grill or the charcoal adds a smoky note to the sausages, and you want your beverage to be able to stand up to that.

This rule also applies to smoked sausages. They have a deeper, more intense smoke flavor so you should pair them with stronger, more intense beers and wines.

Pairing by Garnishes and Condiments

When considering pairing options, think about any garnishes or side dishes you're serving with your sausage, and pair to them. For example, try pairing a chicken and apple sausage with a wine that has aromas of apples or a hard apple cider. Or if you've added green onions to a sausage, find a wine like a Sauvignon Blanc or a sharp ginger beer.

> **CHEF'S CHOICE**
>
> If you're planning to serve your sausage with a tomato sauce, go for an Italian wine like Chianti, which goes great with tomatoes.
>
> If you're planning to serve your sausages with a spicy German mustard, pair them with a nice German beer or a wine that can stand up to the mustard. A Pinot Noir or an unoaked Chardonnay would be a good choice.

A List of Pairing Suggestions

Although certain pairing guidelines have stood the test of time, ultimately, you should use your own tastes to guide you. If you prefer white wines to reds, then serve your sausages with white wines—regardless of whether this goes against certain standard pairing rules. The same goes for beers. If you prefer darker beers, then drink them with your sausage—even if lighter beers are suggested.

However, if you're just not sure what goes with what, you can benefit from the following pairing rules. Here's a list of ten pairings (alphabetical by sausages), as suggested by Jaclyn Stuart, certified sommelier and pairings expert:

- Bratwursts with wheat ales, pilsners, or Pinot Noir (especially German Spatburgunder)

- Chorizo (Mexican) with off-dry Riesling, amber beers, or Vienna lagers

- Chorizo (Spanish) with Tempranillo, Pinotage, or amber beers

- Frankfurters with pilsners, wheat beers, Gewürztraminer, rosé, or drier Riesling

- Game sausages with a porter, stout, Shiraz, or Cabernet Sauvignon

- Italian Sausage with Sangiovese or medium lagers and ales

- Kielbasa with bocks, Marzens, or medium wines (Chenin Blanc and Pinot Noir)

- Poultry sausages with light ales (pale ales and wheat beers), cider, or Chardonnay

- Seafood sausages with pilsners, light ales, Pinot Grigio, or Sauvignon Blanc

- Smoked sausages with Rauchbiers (smoked beers), cask-conditioned ales, Rhone reds, or Shiraz

- Veal sausages with wheat beers, light ales, Chardonnay, or rosé

For more pairing suggestions, check out *The Complete Idiot's Guide to Wine and Food Pairing* (Alpha Books, 2010).

Serving and Entertaining with Sausages

You can make serving and entertaining with sausages as simple or elaborate as you want.

Creating a Sausage Platter

One of the easiest ways to serve sausage is on a sausage platter.

The easiest sausage platter is to make one type of homemade sausage and serve it with a variety of sauces—mustards, mayos, and so on—and a couple of different kinds of buns or breads. This works for any basic type of sausage.

For a more elaborate platter, however, you may do a *horizontal* or a *vertical tasting* of different sausages. A horizontal platter or tasting of sausages is simply a variety of different sausages and condiments—brats, kielbasas, and Italians, for example. A vertical tasting is a more in-depth exploration of one specific type of sausages—a platter of three different German sausages or chorizos, for example.

> **DEFINITION**
>
> A **horizontal tasting** of sausages is a hodgepodge or variety of sausages. A **vertical tasting** of sausages involves two or more sausages of the same style or types.

With a vertical tasting, you might have one or two different condiments, but tailor them specifically to the type of sausage you're focusing on. For example, if you're doing a German tasting, include German mustard and horseradish sauce.

Quality Condiments and Side Dishes

If you've gone to the trouble of making your own sausages, go the extra mile to serve them with quality condiments and sides. You can either make your own (see Chapter 15) or buy high-quality retail brands.

The same goes with the breads or buns you use. Go to a local bakery, and buy bread that enhances the experience of eating your sausages.

You can enhance your sausage platters by adding cheese, vegetables, or fruits. Try to purchase high-quality imported or artisan American cheeses. Since the sausages are the star of the show, opt for cheeses of mild or medium intensity. Aged cheddars, goudas, and fontinas are good choices.

For vegetables, you can serve them as crudités, or you can toss them in simple salads that might accompany the sausages.

Serve fruits in a light fruit salad or prepare them in chutneys or sauces to top your sausages.

Incorporating Sausages into Dishes

When serving your homemade sausages, you can either make them the star of the meal or use them to add a depth of flavor to other dishes. Some traditional dishes like paella, gumbo, or cassoulet put sausages in a starring role (see Chapter 16 for recipes for all three of these entrées).

But you can also incorporate your homemade sausage into other dishes. Toss them into soups and stews for a deeper flavor. Add them to your potpies for an extra savory note.

More importantly, substitute them in anything that calls for ground meat or ground beef. Use your homemade chorizo for tacos, your Italian sausage for lasagnas and pasta sauce, and any kind of sausage for chilis and other soups. Venison sausages and chorizos taste particularly great in chilis—their smoky, spicy nature really enhances their flavors.

Sausages are also great for appetizers. Stuff them in mushrooms, tuck them in empanadas, and add them to crackers with just a dab of mustard or crème fraiche for a simple canapé.

If you're serving brunch, why not create a gourmet breakfast sandwich or add your homemade sausage to breakfast casseroles and quiches? Or simply serve them alongside homemade pancakes or waffles.

If you've made—and frozen—several types of homemade sausages, you can create an entire menu (minus dessert) by incorporating your sausages into different dishes.

The sky's the limit when you cook and entertain with your homemade sausages.

The Least You Need to Know

- Sauté bulk sausages.
- Poach and sauté links, or poach and grill links.
- The easiest rules for pairing sausages with beverages: "goes with where it grows" and "match intensity."
- Sausage platters can be either vertical or horizontal.
- Serve high-quality condiments and foods to get the most out of your homemade sausages.
- Homemade sausages can be used in traditional dishes that call for sausages like cassoulet and gumbo, but they can also enhance tacos and chilis.

Glossary

Appendix A

anaerobic   Without oxygen. An anaerobic environment is one in which there is no oxygen present.

andouille   A type of Cajun or French sausage.

artisan   A food or product that is handcrafted in small batches; also, a person who handcrafts food or products.

BHA   Butylated hydroxyanisole, a preservative that is "reasonably" anticipated to be a human carcinogen, according to the U.S. Department of Health and Human Services.

beef chuck   Cut of meat from the neck and shoulder area of a cow. Also known as *beef shoulder*.

beef shoulder   *See* beef chuck.

botulism   A rare but serious illness that can cause paralysis and death. It is caused by a toxin that's produced by the *Clostridium botulinum* bacterium, which thrives in anaerobic conditions.

boudin blanc   Also called *white boudin*; highly seasoned French sausage that often combines pork with chicken or rabbit and sometimes cereal or rice. Those made in Louisiana are spicier and sometimes contain crawfish.

boudin noir   French sausage containing blood.

bratwurst   German sausage; *brat* means "finely chopped meat" and *wurst* means "sausage."

brine   A salt bath used to preserve or flavor things. Natural casings are usually preserved in brine.

casing   The material that encloses the meat in a linked sausage.

cassoulet   Hearty French casserole.

charcuterie   Store where prepared meats are sold.

charcutier   Someone who prepares cooked meats, especially pork.

chorizo   Spanish word for "sausage."

citric acid   A natural preservative found in citrus fruits.

collagen casing   A sausage casing that's made from the skin of animals.

Community Supported Agriculture (CSA)   A food production and distribution system in which consumers purchase shares of food directly from the farmer before the growing season starts. Then, during the season, the farmer delivers or drops off portions each week.

curing powder   Commercial mix of table salt (sodium chloride), sodium nitrite, and/or sodium nitrate. Sometimes called *curing salt*.

debone   To remove bone from a piece of meat.

fatback pork   A cut of pork taken off the hog's back that is virtually all fat.

five-spice powder   Asian spice blend made of star anise, cloves, cinnamon, Sichuan peppercorns, and either fennel or ginger.

forcemeat   A type of ground meat that's blended with fat.

freezer burn   A condition that occurs when air trapped inside or surrounding a frozen container damages the food inside.

fusion cuisine   A combination of two or more distinct cuisines blended into a single dish or sausage.

galangal   A root in the ginger family that is more peppery than ginger and has a floral, citrusy aroma.

garnish   Ingredients added to sausage after the meat, salt, and spices have been ground.

giardiniera   An Italian pickled vegetable relish.

haggis   A type of Scottish sausage made of organ meats mixed with oatmeal and encased in a sheep's stomach.

horizontal tasting   A sampling of many different kinds of sausages.

jerky gun   A piping tool for making beef jerky that looks like a cookie dough shooter or a pastry gun but is used for meat.

kielbasa   Polish word for "sausage." In the United States, it refers to a specific type of Polish sausage.

kosher salt   Salt that comes in larger-size granules than table salt and most sea salts. It has been blessed by a rabbi.

krakowsa   Sausage made in Poland that is most similar to what Americans know as kielbasa.

linguisa   Portuguese word for "sausage."

locavore   Someone who embraces and tries to eat local foods or foods grown within a 100-mile radius of his or her home.

mis-en-place   French term that means "everything in its place."

monosodium glutamate (MSG)   A food additive that has the ability to intensify the flavor of savory food.

mutton   Sheep over 1 year old.

nitrates and **nitrites**   Naturally occurring chemicals that have nitrogen in them and are added to cured and smoked sausages to prevent botulism.

organic   A practice of farming that produces food naturally, not using synthetic pesticides or fertilizers, and avoids the use of genetically modified organisms. To be considered organic, a product must be certified.

pancetta   A type of Italian bacon made from pork belly that has been cured in spices and then air-dried.

panko   A flaky Japanese breadcrumb made of bread without crusts. It's often used as coating for fried foods such as tempura, but it's also a good substitute in sausage recipes that call for breadcrumbs.

pâté   A spread made of finely minced meat such as liver.

pemmican   A traditional Native American food made from venison or buffalo meat, fat, berries, and herbs packed into containers made out of animal hides.

pork butt   Cut of meat from the top part of a whole pork shoulder; also called *Boston butt* or *pork shoulder*. It is used regularly in sausage.

pork picnic   Cut of meat from below the pork butt or pork shoulder that contains connective tissue and bones; it's sometimes called *shoulder roast*. It is not used in sausage making.

pork shoulder   *See* pork butt.

propyl gallate   A food additive that keeps foods from going rancid if they have a long shelf life.

sake   A rice-based alcoholic beverage.

saltpeter   Also known as the chemical potassium nitrite, it traditionally was used to make cured and smoked sausages. Today, however, sodium nitrite and sodium nitrate are used instead.

salsus   Latin word for "salted," from which the term *sausage* is derived.

Scoville scale   The scale used to measure the amount of heat in a hot pepper.

sea salt   Salt that is harvested from the sea.

shoulder roast   *See* pork picnic.

Slow Food International   An international nonprofit organization that started in Italy. Originally founded in 1986 to protest the establishment of a McDonald's in Rome, this organization embraces and promotes artisan and regional foods.

steel   A rod used to keep the edges of your knives aligned.

table salt   Finely ground salt or sodium chloride. Often called iodized salt, but it does not necessarily contain iodine.

tannins   Bitter compounds found in grape skins, seeds, and stalks that can create a dry, chalky, or puckered feeling in your mouth.

terrine   A meat, fish, or vegetable mixture that has been cooked into a loaf and then cooled and sliced.

terroir   Denotes the effects that geography and distinct environments have on food products, particularly wine and cheese.

texture   The mouthfeel of a food or wine.

trimmings   Extra fat taken from all over the pig.

vegan   Food that contains no dairy, meat, or eggs; also refers to a person who doesn't eat food containing dairy, meat, or eggs.

venison   Typically used to refer to meat of a deer or antelope, but more generally refers to the edible flesh of a game animal.

vertical tasting   A variety of one style or similar types of sausages.

wurst   German word for "sausage."

Sausage Websites

Bratwurst Navigator

www.bratwurstnavigator.de

A German foodie website dedicated to the history and research of bratwurst.

Clifford A. Wright

www.cliffordawright.com

A great source of information on Mediterranean food, culture, and recipes.

Fooducate

www.fooducate.com/blog

A blog that deciphers ingredients lists of foods; it also has an iPhone app.

German Foods

www.germanfoods.org/consumer/facts/guidetosausages.cfm

A great resource for German foods, including German sausages.

Local Harvest

www.localharvest.com

A resource for locating local farmers for purchasing meat and produce.

Meat Processing Products

www.meatprocessingproducts.com

A source for grinders and other meat processing equipment.

Penzeys

www.penzeys.com

An renowned online supplier of spices.

Sausage Maker
www.sausagemaker.com

An online resource for casings and sausage equipment.

Spice House
www.thespicehouse.com

Another great place to order spices.

Wedliny Domowe
www.wedlinydomowe.com

Online presence of a Polish artisan sausage makers organization.

Index

C

Dijon Mustard, 175
drying for smoking, 156
Duck Sausage, 136

E

Eastern European sausage
    Czech Beer Sausage, 96
    Fresh Lithuanian Kielbasa, 93
    Hungarian Kolbasz Sausage, 92
    seasonings, 90
    Serbian Cevapcici Sausage, 94
Eastern European sausage heritage, 89
Easy Dijon Mustard, 175
e. coli, 30
eggs, 63
Elk Sausage, 145
English Sausage Rolls, 202
English sausages. *See* British sausages
environment, safety, 34
equipment
    chef's knife, 25
    cutting boards, 25
    knives
        boning knife, 25
        cutting technique, 42
        holding technique, 41
        maintenance, 25
    measuring spoons, 25
    meat grinder, 26
    mixing bowls/pans, 25
    safety
        grinder, 35-36
        knives, 35
    stuffing appliances, 27
    thermometer, 26
    vacuum sealer, 27, 37
Escoffier, Georges Auguste, 12
exotic ingredients, 118

F

Fancy Breakfast Sausage, 61
fat
    game meats, 19
    pork shoulder/butt, 17
fatback pork, 167
fillers
    breadcrumbs, 63
    eggs, 63
fingernail washing, 31
fire starting for smoking, 157
fish sauce, 122
five-spice powder, 118
flavor enhancers
    salt, 22
    spices, 22-23
flavorings, 5
food preservation, 8
    citric acid, 6
    Han dynasty, 9
    Native Americans, 11
food safety
    equipment, 34-35
    mis-en-place, 32
    sanitation
        clean up procedures, 34
        contact with other items, 34
        cutting boards, 32
        fingernails, 31
        hand washing, 30-31
        head/hair coverings, 31
        importance of, 29
        kitchen counters, 32
        sponges, 32
    storage
        freezing, 37
        transporting, 38
    temperature, 33-34, 152

G

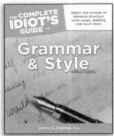

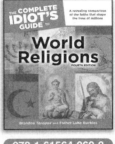
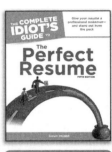
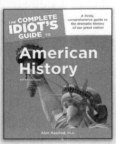
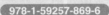

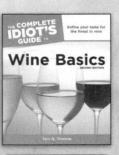